CASE STUDIES IN

CULTURAL ANTHROPOLOGY

GENERAL EDITORS
George and Louise Spindler
STANFORD UNIVERSITY

LAKOTA OF THE ROSEBUD

A Contemporary Ethnography

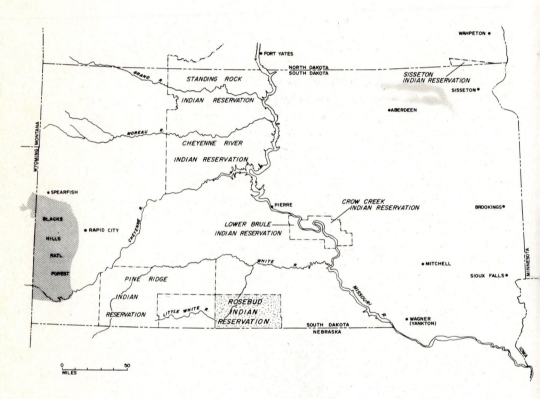

Figure 1. Rosebud and other reservation communities in South Dakota.

LAKOTA OF THE ROSEBUD

A Contemporary Ethnography

by
ELIZABETH S. GROBSMITH
The University of Nebraska—Lincoln

HOLT, RINEHART AND WINSTON
New York   Chicago   San Francisco   Dallas
Montreal   Toronto   London   Sydney

Copyright © 1981 by Holt, Rinehart and Winston

Library of Congress Cataloging in Publication Data

Grobsmith, Elizabeth S
  Lakota of the Rosebud.

  (Case studies in cultural anthropology)
  Bibliography: p.
  1. Brulé Indians. 2. Rosebud Indian Reservation.
I. Title. II. Series.
E99.B8G76   970.004'97   80–39818
ISBN 0–03–057438–2

Manufactured in the United States of America
Published simultaneously in Canada

1 2 3 144 9 8 7 6 5 4 3 2 1

For my mother
MIRIAM E. GROBSMITH
who wanted this

Foreword

ABOUT THE SERIES

These case studies in cultural anthropology are designed to bring to students, in beginning and intermediate courses in the social sciences, insights into the richness and complexity of human life as it is lived in different ways and in different places. They are written by men and women who have lived in the societies they write about and who are professionally trained as observers and interpreters of human behavior. The authors are also teachers, and in writing their books they have kept the students who will read them foremost in their minds. It is our belief that when an understanding of ways of life very different from one's own is gained, abstractions and generalizations about social structure, cultural values, subsistence techniques, and the other universal categories of human social behavior become meaningful.

ABOUT THE AUTHOR

Elizabeth S. Grobsmith is Assistant Professor of Anthropology at the University of Nebraska—Lincoln. She completed her Bachelor of Music at Ohio State University in 1967, but, after taking undergraduate courses in anthropology, decided to pursue graduate work in this field. As an American Jew who spent part of her childhood in Israel, her interests in cultural diversity and minority problems drew her to the study of Native American communities in the United States. With an emphasis on the study of the native cultures of North America, she completed her M.A. (1970) and Ph.D (1976) in anthropology at the University of Arizona in Tucson. Here, she had the opportunity to begin ethnographic fieldwork with the San Carlos Apache of east-central Arizona. Her work with Native Americans continued with participation in a Cross-Cultural Training Program with members of the Sioux tribe for teachers of Indian children in Nebraska schools. After spending the summer of 1973 teaching anthropology at the Sinte Gleska College on the Rosebud Sioux Reservation in South Dakota, she chose Rosebud as the place to conduct her dissertation research on Lakota bilingualism. She lived on the reservation during 1974 and, having completed her research, took a job teaching anthropology at the University of Nebraska. Her interest in the Lakota has continued through the years, resulting in publication of several articles on different aspects of contemporary Indian life. Currently, she is actively involved in research on contemporary Native American life on the Plains.

ABOUT THE BOOK

Ethnographic studies of American Indian tribes and communities have a long history in American anthropology. Many of the long-term preoccupations of American anthropology can be traced to a deep involvement with living Native American cultures, as well as their history and prehistory. Though the popularity of anthropologists with their Native American informants, friends, and collaborators has declined of late due to complex social, ideological, political, and propagandistic events and processes, anthropologists remain the one large professional group who can claim some reliable expertise, on the basis of firsthand contact in the field, about the people and cultures of Native America. They have published prolifically. There is no comparable area of the world about which so much has been written by anthropologists and others, qualified and unqualified, as about native North America.

With the enormous backlog of published material available, one asks why another book? The answer is in this case study. American Indians and their cultures have not remained static. North America before the coming of Europeans was a dynamic, changing area of the world, and changes were accelerated by contact with the West. Though many populations of Native Americans were nearly obliterated by alien diseases against which they had no immunities, to say nothing of murder and genocide, many of them have now rebounded to greater numbers than at any time since the midnineteenth century. And though the "white man" made every effort to stamp out the indigenous cultures of North America through religious proselytizing and assimilationist education as well as military, economic and political means, the cultures, too, have survived, though much changed.

What Elizabeth Grobsmith writes about is the complex, adapting cultures of the Lakota Sioux reservation community. It is not merely a community within which some interesting remnants of the "traditional" culture survive. Nor is it a community where everybody speaks English, where no one has ever ridden a horse or lived in a tipi, and the traditional culture is just a whisper from the past, a dead past. Nor is it a community somewhere in between the past and the present. It is a community of variety and adaptation. It is not possible to say "Lakota Sioux," or "Rosebud Reservation" and have these terms stand for a single, homogeneous people, place, or set of conditions. This case study lays out succinctly what life is like today among the Lakota, and why it is that way—in its many variations.

GEORGE AND LOUISE SPINDLER
General Editors

Calistoga, California

Other case studies edited by George and Louise Spindler devoted to Native North America that the reader should find interesting and useful are listed at the end of this case study.

Preface

The Sioux are probably one of the best documented tribes in native North America. Unlike many tribes whose language and culture are only vaguely known, nearly every aspect of Lakota life—ritual, tradition, language—has been recorded and preserved. From this rich literature as well as from popularized media on the Sioux, the public has formed images of brave buffalo hunters, the mighty warriors of the Plains. Although, like most tribes, the Lakota at Rosebud no longer live the same life style they did a century ago, their culture is by no means gone. Rather, it has thrived, evolved, and met the challenge of living in the twentieth century in a unique and interesting way.

It is unfortunate that we have come to regard and categorize native cultures as either purely traditional and therefore dying or as assimilated and consequently less pure and interesting. In reality, contemporary native culture is a blending of both traditional and modern elements. Today, both reservation and urban Indians choose to retain certain features of their native culture while simultaneously adopting aspects of western life. But the adoption of these new elements has not necessarily meant the rejection of native tradition.

The time has come to examine and appreciate the contemporary life of Indian people, in this case, life as a Lakota at Rosebud. By doing this, stereotypic impressions of life in Plains tribal groups can be dispelled. We want to understand what Indian society has become after a century of intense cultural exchange.

This case study is a contemporary view of the Brule band of Teton Lakota who have become the Rosebud Sioux Tribe of South Dakota. All of the Lakota at Rosebud—mixed-bloods as well as full-bloods—express in their daily living, religious worship, and beliefs a cultural style that is a mixture of native tradition, Christian influences, and western economic technology and pressures. The result is a unique culture: traditional for some, apparently totally westernized for others. For the majority, it is a combination, a blending, a distinctly Indian style or interpretation for nearly every reservation event. Here, then, is a brief picture of Rosebud as it is today.

ACKNOWLEDGMENTS

I am grateful to my parents, Michael and Miriam Grobsmith, for their financial and emotional support, particularly during the fieldwork period. My husband and colleague, Professor James A. Gibson, provided stimulating and thoughtful assistance with the Lakota ethnography as well as with editorial aspects of the book. Mrs. Pat Friesen read and commented on earlier drafts and provided very useful insights. Kate Simon kindly allowed me to profit from her skill as a writer by making editorial suggestions. I am also grateful to my friend and colleague, Professor Daniela Weinberg, for her painstaking editorial assistance. In addition, I would like to thank Mrs. Dorothy McEwen for her expert typing and unending patience in keeping up with revisions. She made my task much easier. I am grateful to Dr. Peter Bleed of the Department of Anthropology and to Mr. Carl Falk of the Division of Archeological Research at the University of Nebraska for providing support to assist in the completion of this book, and to Ms. Sally Donovan who skillfully drew the maps and illustrations. Nancy Higgins, my friend and field assistant, helped immeasurably by devoting six weeks' time to the research. I appreciate her assistance and companionship.

The University of Nebraska Research Council provided me with a Junior Faculty Summer Research Fellowship during the summer of 1979 to enable me to devote my full energies to completion of the manuscript. I would like to express my gratitude for their support.

To the Lakota of the Rosebud go my heartfelt thanks for permitting me to invade the privacy of their lives and have the privilege of participating in their culture. It has enriched my life considerably. I am grateful to Mr. Robert Burnette, 1974 chairman of the Rosebud Sioux Tribe, for permission to conduct research on the reservation. A number of individuals were especially helpful to me in obtaining information about modern Lakota concerns: Mr. Opie La Pointe of the Rosebud Housing Authority; Mr. Frank Pommersheim of the Sinte Gleska College; Mr. Hubert McCloskey, realty specialist in the BIA Branch of Natural Resources; Mr. Charles Owens, natural resources officer in the Branch of Natural Resources and Mr. Bruce Pretty Bird of the Tribal Planning Office. Their assistance is gratefully acknowledged.

I would like to thank Mr. Gerald Mohatt, director of the Community Mental Health Project at Sinte Gleska College, for the time and effort he spent going through the manuscript. His suggestions for its improvement reflect the great care he took to correct inaccuracies, clear up ambiguities, and develop ideas he felt would more correctly represent the Lakota people. I am also grateful to Mr. Victor Douville, chairman of the Lakota Department at Sinte Gleska, for reading and working on the manuscript. His insight and deep understanding of Lakota life, especially in the area of native religion, provided a valuable perspective I could not otherwise have gained.

Mr. Opie La Pointe and Mr. Charles Owens read portions of the manuscript and provided clarification and editorial assistance. I appreciate the time they took in assisting in the completion of the manuscript.

I would also like to thank special friends on the reservation who helped, not only with the research, but also with making my experiences at Rosebud rich and meaningful: the Blue Thunder family—Mabel, Rose, Leo and Vernie, Jr., Muriel Bierle, Beth and Lorenzo Black Lance, and Elaine Left Hand Bull, now deceased.

E.G.

Contents

CASE STUDIES IN

CULTURAL ANTHROPOLOGY

GENERAL EDITORS
George and Louise Spindler
STANFORD UNIVERSITY

LAKOTA OF THE ROSEBUD

A Contemporary Ethnography

1 / Getting started at Rosebud

In 1973 when I embarked on a course for doing field research for a Ph.D. dissertation, I had no idea that I would discover an area . . . a place . . . a people . . . who would, for all time, change my life. For most anthropologists entering "the field," there are so many concerns and preparations that one rarely has time to sit back and ponder what events will occur in the next year's time. Having made the decision to study language use on the Rosebud Sioux Reservation, I began to arrange for permission to conduct my study. I contacted the Office of the Tribal Council Chairman and explained fully my intentions and the ways in which I hoped my research would be of some benefit to the Lakota at Rosebud. After nearly six months with no reply, I wrote again, and this time received a letter giving me the official sanction of the tribe to begin my work. It wasn't until I was well along in my research that I learned that *having* Tribal Council permission was not necessarily an advantage. Due to conflicting political opinion, some tribal members felt that my having "official" permission was fine, but others complained of political corruption, telling me that this official body could not and did not represent them. I began to get a glimmer of the complexity and tremendous heterogeneity of the reservation population—something I had not known before.

Getting settled on a reservation is no easy task, especially when rumors of dangers to non-Indian outsiders abound. I was aware that the American Indian Movement had been active at Rosebud, and that, only a year after the 1973 occupation of Wounded Knee, Indian sentiment was definitely on making significant economic and political changes. I was uncertain how welcome a white, female anthropology graduate student would be, especially one who had come "to study the Indians." Deloria's book *Custer Died for Your Sins* (1969) was very popular, and the image of the anthropologist—well-intentioned or not—was not exactly that of a welcomed savior.

As aware and wide-eyed as could be, my field assistant and I set out for Rosebud and found temporary lodging in a motel, while we searched for housing. We were not aware that a skirmish had occurred earlier in the day between AIM (American Indian Movement) and the FBI. We had heard a rumor that AIM had machine guns set up on tripods and were shooting at all cars with out-of-state license plates, which my car had. We didn't encounter any guns, but at 3:00 A.M. someone nearly pounded our door down looking for various AIM members who were supposedly in hiding. In the morning, we learned that it had been the FBI beating on the

1

doors at the motel! My field assistant thought our "welcome" (or lack of it) was a clear message to get out—but after all the plans and arrangements we had made, folding up and running away was not exactly a good response to the challenge. We decided to draw in a deep breath and go exploring.

Finding housing on a reservation is such a near-insurmountable obstacle that many people change their minds and move to a nearby town like Valentine, Nebraska, or Winner, South Dakota. So little housing is available for the Indians that there are long waiting lists to qualify for a house. Legally only Indians are entitled to live in the housing projects, since they are part of federally funded housing developments. Knowing that anthropologists must truly "live in the community" in order to be close to the routines of daily life, we searched relentlessly and, after spending a week in the Todd County High School boarding facilities, finally located a cabin in the town of Mission on the reservation. It had three rooms, but heat in only one. My field assistant and I divided up the bed; I took the mattress and she slept on the box spring. It may not have been fancy, but for the next seven months, it was to be home.

At first, Indians and non-Indians alike could not understand why I would want to move there to do research. Some were perplexed that I should move to Rosebud to "work" when they didn't see me out looking for a job. The non-Indians asked, "Why do you want to study the Indians?" and the Lakota asked, "Why do you want to study *us*?" I had been warned that the Lakota might be unreceptive to my project and unresponsive to me. What I discovered could not have been more the opposite. Not only were the Indian people helpful, cooperative, and interested in participating in my research, but they were delighted that their knowledge—their language—was considered by an outsider to be "worth studying."

In the months that followed, my adventures were many and varied. As with all fieldworkers, there are special and memorable times. Relationships form that do not end when the research has been completed. In many ways, the Lakota are a people who "take you in," care for you, and treat you as kin. They share with you what they have and are willing to talk with you about what they know and feel.

It would be untrue to say that all of my experiences at Rosebud were pleasant. With Indians friends and neighbors, as with others, one experiences violent, unnecessary deaths; severe, disrupting alcoholism; abject poverty; and for some, a total loss of self. The feelings one is left with are frustration and confusion about why these situations have developed, and about what can be done to correct them.

Although I originally went to Rosebud to study language, I became interested in so many facets of contemporary Native American life that I began to explore many different questions: Why did some communities appear "traditional" while others seemed to reject links to the past? What role did Christianity play in the lives of these people, and how did the unique blend of Christian and native beliefs come about? How strong was the Native American (Peyote) Church? Why did so few Lakota own their own businesses, and what was being done to train the Lakota for business management? How did the Lakota view the American Indian Movement and its radical ideas? Why was bilingual education an interesting prospect for some communities, and an impossibility for others? What could be

This scene captures the blend of traditional and western elements so typical of Rosebud today.

done about alcoholism, underemployment, highway deaths? And more importantly, how had these people managed to retain so many of their native beliefs and values in the face of such tremendous acculturative pressures?

I became intensely interested in the fact that although on the surface reservation life appeared to be largely western, a uniquely Lakota attitude, philosophy, and value system pervaded everything. Although assimilation had occurred on one level —in the use of western technology and so forth—it had not occurred at a deeper level. What was the result of the adoption of a western style of life while personal goals and motivations derived their meaning from a different—a native—set of precepts? What adjustments did (and do) Lakota make to accommodate the dominant society's rules? And to what extent were contemporary problems such as alcoholism a result of this juxtaposition of two rather radically different traditions?

I found that the compromise made in living as an Indian in today's world was different for different individuals, and that any representation of Lakota life as uniform could not be valid. I discovered people who lived as their ancestors did, with few of the comforts of modern conveniences, such as central heating, refrigeration, or plumbing. Others I met held eight to five jobs, earned steady incomes, and sent their children to college. Some were strict Catholics or Episcopalians. Others practiced native rituals and shunned "the white man's religion." Some children spoke their native Lakota language with fluent ease; others learned how to count from one to ten in Indian Studies classes at school. The amount and way in which Lakota culture varied—among individuals as well as communities—was staggering. Whatever questions I was able to figure out about part of the population certainly did not apply to the remainder.

With my research completed, I left Rosebud, with eagerness to begin a new job and equal regret about leaving a people I had learned to admire, respect, and love. In the years since I have left, I have returned often, both to visit and to participate in the celebrations and daily events of the culture. Each time I returned, I felt that the distance I gained had helped me achieve some deeper insight into what I had learned and experienced. And each time I returned, my questions increased, and my frustrations about reservation problems grew.

The reservation "situation"—if there is such a thing—is a complex puzzle that consists of numerous interlocking pieces. The overwhelming heterogeneity of the Lakota people makes the puzzle especially difficult to piece together, but especially interesting as well.

This case study represents my attempt to "make sense" of modern Lakota life, to try to characterize the Lakota as they really are today rather than perpetrate images of wild equestrian warriors who ride around hunting buffalo and living in tipis. The Lakota are survivors. They have endured years of prejudice, hatred, and genocide. They have overcome political obstacles and have resisted total assimilation. Today, they reflect every attitude and style of the Native American experience and they fit everywhere along the continuum, which ranges from strictly indigenous or traditional to fully assimilated. Most Lakota are somewhere in between. But one thing is constant, and that is the strong sense of pride in being a Native American, and an even stronger sense of identity in being Lakota. Perhaps this book can bring the world of the Lakota a little more into focus than it has been, and can give the student of the American Indian a greater depth, appreciation, and knowledge of what it means to be an Indian today.

2/ A brief history of the Rosebud Sioux

2.1 ARRIVAL AND SETTLEMENT ON THE PLAINS

In contrast with many Native American tribes whose historical legends indicate an ancient association with a particular territory, the Lakota of the Rosebud Reservation are recent comers to the Plains. The Lakota, or Sioux, as they are more commonly known, are part of the western or Teton division of Sioux. The word *Sioux* is not a native term but was applied to them by the Chippewa and means the "Lesser Adders" (snakes) or *Nadoweisiw-eg.* The Chippewa used this term to distinguish these people from their more threatening neighbors, the Iroquois, whom they called the "True Adders." The French, unable to pronounce the Chippewa term, shortened it to *Sioux,* the designation by which they have been known ever since. The Sioux at Rosebud call themselves Lakota—a term that refers both to their tribal identity and the language they speak. Lakota is a dialect of the "Dakota Sioux" language within the Siouan linguistic family. The other two dialects—Nakota, spoken by the northern or Yankton Sioux, and Dakota (proper), spoken by the eastern or Santee Sioux—are mutually intelligible with Lakota.

The area into which the Sioux roamed was a vast plain stretching from Saskatchewan south to Texas and from the Missouri River west to the Rocky Mountains. This vast grassland supported two rather distinct and specialized types of cultures. In the western region, a rather dry, short-grass area, roamed nomadic hunters who, first on foot and later on horseback, pursued the bison herds that grazed throughout the area. The eastern portion or tall-grass prairie was, and had been for a thousand years, the home of tribes who farmed in the rich bottomland of permanently flowing rivers that emptied into the Missouri. The Upper Missouri tribes were settled into large stable villages; they flourished in this wetter, more lush environment and, at the time of the arrival of the Lakota, had been living peacefully in a region rich with game, timber, and ample water for their crops. To the north lived the Siouan Mandan and Hidatsa tribes; their neighbors to the south were the Caddoan-speaking Arikara and Pawnee. Contrary to stereotypic notions of the Plains as a great American desert virtually uninhabited before the coming of the nomadic tribes, the area into which the Lakota migrated was occupied, settled, and under the control of long-established cultures. With the migration of the Sioux, as well as other hunting tribes, into the area, Indian life on the Plains was never to be the same.

5

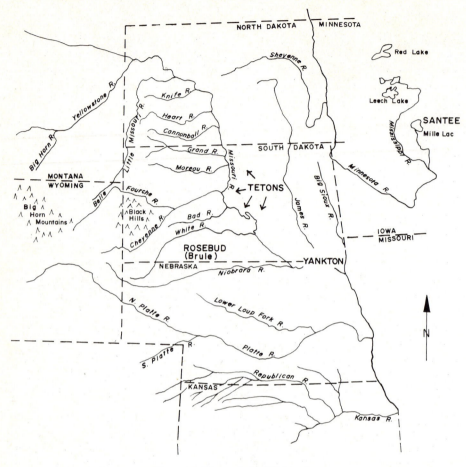

Figure 2. Map of the Plains Area

The Sioux, who became famous hunters and warriors in this Plains region, originally came from the prairie zone to the east, a mixed grassland and forested area near present-day central Minnesota. They were seen by Jesuits in the Great Lakes region near Lake Superior as early as 1641 before their migration to the Plains, but relatively little is known about their culture prior to their later contact with explorers and traders. By 1750 they had wandered in small bands in search of food following the buffalo herds out onto the Plains. They hunted in the Upper Minnesota River Valley, along the Missouri River, and along the James River, finally settling in the region of the White River in present-day South Dakota. By the time they arrived on the Plains, they had already organized themselves into the tribal divisions by which we know them today.

The Seven Council Fires

When they made their descent onto the Plains, all the Sioux tribes constituted a political unit called the Očeti Šakowin or "Seven Council Fires." (See Figure 3.)

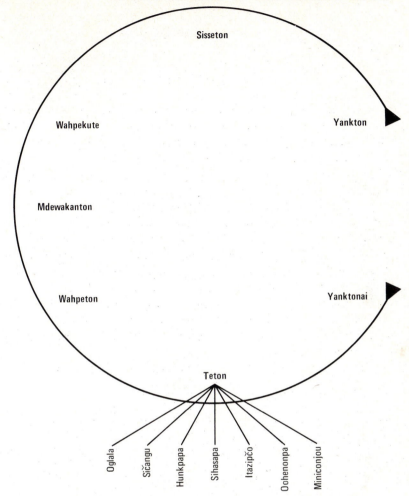

Figure 3. Camp Circle of the Seven Council Fires

It consisted of seven major divisions. The largest division was called the Teton or western Sioux (from *tetonwan*, meaning "dwellers of the prairie") and it consisted of seven smaller bands. The division next in size was the Santee or eastern Sioux (from *isanti*, meaning "knife," and referring to their settlement at Knife Lake, Minnesota). There were four distinct tribes within the Santee division: the Wahpeton ("dwellers among the leaves"), the Mdewakanton ("people of Spirit Lake"), the Wahpekute ("shooters among the leaves"), and Sisseton ("camping among the swamps"). The last and smallest division was the Yankton or northern division (from *ihanktunwan*, meaning "dwellers on the end"), which consisted of two tribes, the Ihanktunwan proper (or "Yankton") and the Ihanktunwanna (or Yanktonai, meaning "little Yankton").

The Teton division of Sioux was the first to cross the Missouri River and take on the lifestyle that came to characterize all the Sioux—that of nomadic bison hunters. Although they were similar culturally and spoke a common language, they were organized into seven separate bands, which have remained distinct to this day. The largest band was the Oglala ("they scatter their own"), who now reside on the Pine Ridge Reservation. Next in size was the Sičangu ("burnt thigh") or Brule (also meaning "burnt") band, who now live on the Rosebud, Lower Brule, and Crow Creek Reservations. An event recorded in a winter count of 1762–63 explains how the Sičangu or Brule got their name:

> The band was encamped on the shore of one of the long, narrow lakes that are a feature of the country in Eastern South Dakota. The grass of the prairie caught fire. A man, his wife, and some children, who were out on the prairie, were burned to death; the rest of the Sioux saved themselves by leaping into the lake; but most of the Indians had their legs and thighs badly burnt, and ugly scars resulted. The band was therefore given the new name of "Sichangu" or Burnt Thighs. The French traders termed them Brules (Hyde 1974:5).

The five remaining bands of Teton Lakota included the Hunkpapa ("those who camp at the entrance"), Sihasapa ("blackfeet"), Itazipčo ("without bows," also known as the Sans Arcs), Oohenonpa ("two boilings" or "two kettles"), and Miniconjou ("those who plant by the stream"). These smaller bands live on the Lower Brule, Standing Rock, and Cheyenne River Reservations in South Dakota.

During most of the year the members of the Seven Council Fires neither hunted nor lived together. Once a year all the divisions came together for the celebration of the annual Sun Dance ceremony, followed by the fall buffalo hunt. Unlike the regular pattern of hunting in small groups, the annual hunt was highly organized and regimented. It was policed by certain societies, which enforced strict rules and guidelines for this major event. After the hunt, the seven divisions returned to their separate locations and did not reunite for another full year.

Settlement on the Plains

The western or Teton tribes crossed the Missouri around 1750, reaching as far west as the Black Hills by 1765. By 1800 they had a relatively fixed residence along the White and Bad Rivers in present-day South Dakota, where they were seen by Lewis and Clark in 1804. Hyde describes their arrival in "Rosebud" country (named for the wild rose plant):

> The White River country of southern South Dakota, into which the Brules wandered after crossing the Missouri, was probably the finest tract of land for Indian occupation west of and close to the Missouri. A real Indian paradise, it was a land full of buffalo and other game, with a topography that gave the Indians open plains and prairies on which to hunt, many fine streams with groves of timber in which to camp, and pine ridges from which timber for lodgepoles and other uses could easily be obtained. There were vast areas of the finest native pasture on which to fatten their ponies in summer, and a plentiful supply of sweet cottonwood along the streams, which provided bark for feeding ponies in winter (1961:5).

The country they inhabited was ideal. They had a permanent supply of water, ample timber, and a prairie teeming with game—buffalo, antelope, deer, and elk. Their proximity to the Missouri allowed them to obtain trade items upon which they had become increasingly dependent: guns, ammunition, steel axes, and iron kettles. By 1800, the White River was "in the undisputed possession of the Brules" (Hyde 1974:12). During the next fifty years, more bands of Sioux arrived from the east to share the prosperous life with the Brules. With the increase in population the Sioux began to dominate the area, becoming a menace to the village tribes, who were prior occupants of the area. They roamed into the Sand Hills region of Nebraska and captured many horses from wild herds. To supplement their herds, the Sioux raided the Pawnee, a Caddoan-speaking horticultural tribe who lived in permanent earth lodges on the Loup Fork branch of the Lower Platte. In all ways, the Sioux prospered—and since it was largely at the expense of other tribes, they quickly gained a reputation as hostile predators.

The horse, originally brought to North America by the Spaniards, was brought to the Plains by two routes: along the eastern edge of the Rockies through the Nez Perce and Shoshone tribes, and from the southern Plains through the Comanche, Cheyenne, and Arapahoe. Horses were traded by Indians on the Upper Missouri long before most Indians had ever seen a white trader.

The horse totally revolutionized the Lakota way of life. It transformed the Lakota from a loose aggregate of small bands that wandered in search of food, to an organized and powerful society. The significance of the horse was evident even in the name they gave it—*šunka wakan,* "sacred dog." Acquisition of the horse affected nearly every aspect of the culture: it replaced the dog as the principal beast of burden; it enabled them to have greater mobility and cover a much wider territory more quickly, resulting in a greater exploitation of game and exhaustion of local resources. Hunting the buffalo was a task more easily accomplished on horseback. The horse's efficiency insured a bountiful supply of food. But more meat than necessary could easily be obtained and the size of the herds was reduced quickly. Roaming over vast stretches of prairie, the Lakota came into contact with tribes with whom they developed hostile relationships, such as the Crow, Shoshone, Pawnee, and Arikara.

Horses became a medium of exchange, an item of value against which the price of other goods was determined. They were used as payment for goods: for example, the purchase price of a shield or war bonnet was one horse. Horses were also used as payment for services rendered—a horse might be given for having a child's ears pierced or as a reward for a particular feat or favor, such as helping a Sun Dancer break free of his bonds. Because of their durability and value, horses became highly prized gifts. They were used to gain entrance into societies otherwise closed to membership; they were also given during the Giveaway ceremony or at a girl's puberty rite. Horses were the most common item of exchange in marriage: "A young man usually arranged to give horses and gifts to the girl's family in order that he might be regarded as a reputable person" (Hassrick 1964:126).

Horses became tangible evidence of the accumulation of wealth and symbols of prestige. In order to obtain economic security as well as higher status it became necessary to supplement one's herds. This was done by stealing or capture, which were considered acts of valor in themselves. Capturing horses required a great deal of skill. The incentive for a successful raid was not only the economic benefit, but the prestige acquired if the mission was successful.

> Raiding enemy villages was the foundation upon which the economic system rested—it was the key to individual success and group wealth (Hassrick 1964: 91).

Material wealth achieved through capturing horses had substantial effects on Lakota society; affluence became possible and a previously egalitarian society began to develop classlike distinctions based on the new level of prosperity. Although these were not fixed, rigid classes, increase in wealth gave certain individuals an important role in society, one that contributed toward the benefit of the entire group.

In addition, the horse had become a religious symbol: "It possessed the attributes of supernatural potency, analogous to 'medicine'" (Hassrick 1964:183). It gave the Lakota an advantage, not only in hunting, but in the spiritual realm as well. Without the horse, the Sioux would never have gained the reputation as "mystic warriors of the Plains":

> There is every reason to believe that the Sioux could not have survived the rigors of the plains without the buffalo, and there is good reason to believe that population by hunting groups could not have existed without the horse (Hassrick 1964:189).

Once the horse became an integral part of life, the Lakota spent a considerable amount of time protecting their new claims and defending their new territories. They engaged regularly in warfare, not only as a means of protecting their gains, but for its own sake as an expression of Sioux bravery and valor. The Sioux obtained guns at the trade centers on the Missouri and depended on them in hostile acts of raiding, retaliation, and conquest. They journeyed to the trade centers more often as the need for ammunition and supplies became more urgent. By 1830, warfare had been woven into the fabric of Lakota life to the extent that gaining war honors became an end in itself. Striking an enemy ("counting coup") was the basis of the war honor system. Points were assigned for touching—not killing—the enemy. The daring required in this close contact—courting danger and risking death—was the basis for honors given. This and other acts of bravery became the best avenue for achieving prestige and high status.

The convergence of the horse and the gun on the Plains had a dramatic effect on the Sioux and their interactions with other tribes. On horseback they wielded considerable power over their newly acquired territory, dominating the villages, whose enemy they had become. They roamed north to the villages of the Arikara—Caddoan-speaking relatives of the Pawnee—and demanded exchange of their goods for corn, plundering when they could not force the exchange. They maintained exclusive control over trade on the Missouri River, harrassing Indians and traders alike. The powerful, conquering Sioux reigned over the northern Plains and gained a reputation—and a well-deserved one at that—as fierce hunters and warriors. These were the mounted warriors who became the stereotyped High Plains Indian. But their control was short-lived.

By 1850, most of the resources on which the Sioux depended were exhausted; one district after another had been hunted out. Groves of trees had been ruined by fire and bark-cutting to feed the ponies. Pressure from French fur traders brought even greater destruction: the traders had created a profitable market for buffalo robes

and salted tongues. The Sioux were slaughtering huge numbers of buffalo to supply the ever-increasing demands of this market. Hunting for trade rather than
for subsistence, the Sioux were now engaged full-time as traders and were becoming increasingly dependent on European goods. Visiting the trading centers regularly, they came into contact with alcohol continuously. Liquor was being used
by traders as a bribe to keep the Sioux loyal to specific trading companies, and
its effects on the Sioux were devastating: "The Brules had become split up and
disorganized by the heavy drinking of the 1820's" (Hyde 1974:26). By 1830, the
Brule bands dispersed due to the reduced number of buffalo on the Plains. Some
Brule followed the herds moving south to the Platte River. These bands became
known as the Upper Brules or "people away from the Missouri River" (Hyde
1974:36). It was this division that eventually became the Rosebud Sioux. The
remaining Brules continued to camp on the White River and retained their trade
relationships on the Missouri. They became known as the "lowland people" or
Lowland Brules. This division of Sioux eventually became the Lower Brule of the
Lower Brule Reservation in South Dakota.

By the 1850s the sedentary village tribes along the Missouri had been decimated
by diseases introduced by traders. The Brules visited the river trade centers
regularly and came increasingly into contact with smallpox and measles carried
by traders; they returned to their people carrying the diseases. Immigrants heading
west to California and Oregon brought new epidemics, further reducing native
populations.

By 1850—one hundred years after their arrival on the Plains—the Sioux had
been stripped of their political powers and were forced to yield to demands of the
encroaching white settlers and their government. Disease, alcohol, and the struggle
over land took their toll on the Lakota.

2.2   THE LAKOTA AND THE U.S. GOVERNMENT

After a century and a half on the Plains, the Sioux way of life was radically
transformed. From 1851—the year of the signing of the Fort Laramie Treaty, the
first of a long series of treaties involving the Sioux—until 1878, the Sioux "moved
from the dominant position in their area to that of a defeated nation living on
reservations established by the United States government" (Spicer 1969:84). Before 1851, they roamed freely from the Upper Missouri down to what is now the
state of Arkansas, including all of present-day South Dakota west of the Missouri
and east of the Big Horn Mountains. The Fort Laramie Treaty reduced their original
territory and assigned them a homeland, enclosed by the Heart, Missouri, White,
and North Platte Rivers, and the Black Hills.

The Treaty of 1868 established the Great Sioux Reservation and delineated the
boundaries within which the Sioux were permitted to roam: between the northern
and southern South Dakota borders and west of the Missouri River. This treaty
guaranteed that Indian land was to be "entered only with Indian consent and
affirmed that the Sioux would cease raiding" (Spicer 1969:85). The discovery of
gold in the Black Hills brought prospectors and more settlers to South Dakota, who,

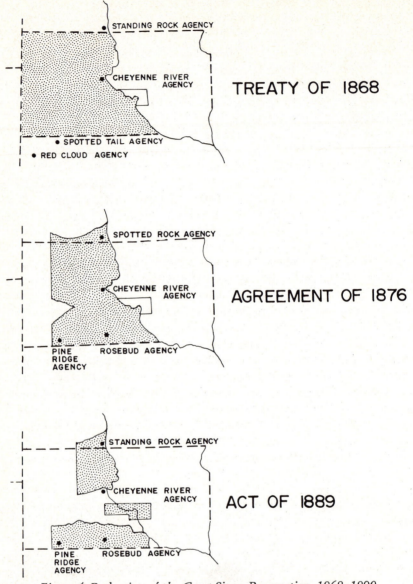

Figure 4. Reduction of the Great Sioux Reservation, 1868–1890
Source: Utley (1963)

despite the stipulations of the treaty, began to settle on reservation land. The Sioux were angered by the disregard for the treaty and led hostile, retaliatory raids on the settlers. The result was military defeat of the Sioux and their forced surrender. Spicer describes the events:

> The U.S. chopped the Black Hills from Sioux country. . . . One by one, the Sioux bands were defeated, Crazy Horse's Oglala band surrendering in 1877 and Gall

and Sitting Bull of the Tetons in 1881. . . . As the last fighting bands surrendered they were put on reservations in South Dakota, some on the Rosebud Reservation under Spotted Tail and others at Pine Ridge under Red Cloud (Spicer 1969:85).

This further reduction of their territory—from half the state of South Dakota in 1868 to small individual agencies at Rosebud, Pine Ridge, Cheyenne River, and Standing Rock by 1889—resulted in the collapse of Sioux land holdings. (See Figure 4.) Instead of one vast reservation, the Sioux were scattered on small land tracts. Various chiefs were given the opportunity to select their own sites for their new agencies. Chief Red Cloud of the Oglala chose Pine Ridge; Chief Spotted Tail chose the site of Rosebud. Despite much objection by Indian commissioners, the selection of Rosebud as the agency was finally approved. In November of 1877 the Brule Sioux, under Spotted Tail's leadership, were relocated there. Rosebud's boundaries were officially fixed on February 28, 1877, and the agency was established in 1878. Today Rosebud is still the agency town for the reservation, the link between the federal government and the entire reservation community.

Once the reservation boundaries had been firmly established, another major act of legislation was passed that was to have further drastic consequences for tribal holdings. The Allotment or Dawes Severalty Act of 1887 was passed in the hope that, by dividing reservation holdings into individually held allotments, the system of tribal ownership would be undermined and the native culture would break down. The Allotment Act was based on the notion that Indian reservations were an obstacle to the encroaching white civilization. Assimilation of the unwanted Indians into a white lifestyle was the best solution. Assimilation was to be accomplished by teaching the white values of pride and self-sufficiency in individual land ownership. Once the land was allotted, stock-raising and farming were to be introduced and the Sioux transformed into independent ranchers. During the transition, rations were to be distributed to tide people over until they were self-sufficient.

Despite the government's intention, no individual was permitted to own his

The agency town of Rosebud is the central location of tribal and BIA offices and hospital facilities.

land outright. Allotments were held in trust for a period of twenty-five years. After that, the title could be obtained if the allottee was deemed "competent." The Burke Act of 1906 allowed the waiting period to be waived. The Secretary of the Interior could issue a patent to any allottee judged competent. But it was not until 1934 and the passage of the Indian Reorganization Act that an Indian person could obtain the title to his land without a waiting period.

The provisions for carrying out assimilation were included in the Treaty of 1868—nearly a decade before the Allotment Act: The Sioux were furnished with "25,000 cows and 1000 bulls, oxen, farming tools, a two-year supply of seeds for five acres" (Utley 1963:45). The Indians initially resisted government efforts to induce them to "scratch the ground." They were encouraged to farm by the government "boss farmers" assigned to each reservation district. These men not only taught farming techniques, but also controlled the issue of beef—killed, butchered, and issued at selected issue stations. Beef was issued in hopes of keeping the people from leaving the reservation in search of meat. The manner of issuing beef was itself an inducement for the Sioux to comply with these restraints:

> In the earlier years of the beef issue the cattle were turned loose on the prairie and the Indians shot them from horseback somewhat like a buffalo hunt. It offered diversion as well as meat, and the Indian families would then skin and dress the animal out on the prairie where it fell. This was discontinued because with the cattle running loose, and so many people present, there was too much likelihood of someone getting shot. After some Indians were shot the practice was changed. Of course the authorities also wanted them to change to the white man's way (Anderson 1971:98).

Other rations included bacon, rice, navy beans, flour, baking powder, sugar, green coffee, clothing, and laundry soap.

Farming was precarious in the dry, sandy area. Besides, stock-raising had more appeal to the Lakota. Cattle-ranching grew in importance during the twenty-year period since the reservation had been established at Rosebud. But it was interrupted in 1887 by the new plan to parcel out reservation land to individuals.

The Allotment Act of 1887 was instrumental in breaking up the Great Sioux Reservation. It called for the division of land into 160-acre allotments per family. The Sioux resisted allotment and were unfavorably disposed to this scheme. Two years later the Sioux Act of 1889 was passed (see Figure 4); it was designed to make allotment more acceptable to the Sioux. Instead of the 160-acre allotment, family heads would receive 320 acres; single persons over eighteen and orphans under eighteen were to receive 80-acre allotments. The Sioux were offered the right to amalgamate their land in order to facilitate grazing as an incentive to accepting the allotment. No allotment was to begin until a majority of adult males on the reservation accepted it. As a final threat, the Sioux were told their rations would be cut off if they did not cooperate with allotment. In 1889, the first Lakota accepted an allotment, made official in 1890. Those who held out altogether and refused to accept allotments soon found their rations cut off. One Brule leader, Crow Dog, "did not accept an allotment until 1910, exactly twenty years after the first allotment had been made in 1890" (Anderson 1971:273). For many Indians it was a choice between accepting allotment or starving. In the period between 1898 and 1900 the greatest number of allotments were made on the Rosebud Reservation—nearly 2 million acres of reservation land had been parceled out to individuals (Ballas 1970).

The combination of events during the allotment period left the Sioux vulnerable to and dependent on the U.S. government. This dependent relationship, once necessary for survival, resulted in growing bitterness and hatred between the Indians and the government. By the late 1880s the buffalo had nearly become extinct. Once the railroads were constructed, the remaining herds were permanently divided and dispersed. Dependence on the buffalo, even if permitted, became impossible. Thus the dependence on government-issued rations grew. But although the rations had been promised until the Lakota could become self-sufficient, there were periods during which these supplies were totally cut off. In 1889, rations were "cut off in accordance with the treaty, and no adequate provision was made for food" (Spicer 1969:86). Utley describes the utter despair common among the Indians at the time:

> The land agreement shook the Teton tribes with more violence than anything in their history, and it threw into sharp focus the resentments and frustrations built up in a decade of reservation life. The winter of 1889–90—with unrelieved hunger, disastrous epidemics, the opening of the ceded lands . . . emptied the Tetons of hope (Utley 1963:60).

By the end of the allotment period, most reservations had been drastically reduced in size. After parceling out land to individuals, the remaining land was declared "surplus." Throughout the United States a total of 91 million acres of once Indian land was opened for sale to non-Indians. "Of an original area of 3,228,161 acres, the Rosebud Reservation had lost 2,195,905 acres by 1934 through sales, lands ceded to the U.S. Government and 'miscellaneous land losses' " (Ballas 1970: 42). Since individual landholders could also sell their allotments and were encouraged to do so, reduction of an Indian land base—the government's ultimate goal—was accomplished.

In hopes of completing the assimilation process, the church and the federal government together constructed Indian schools to instill western values in children, to teach the English language, and generally to separate the Sioux from their indigenous tradition. In 1874 the first boarding school was established on the Rosebud reservation. The Roman Catholic mission, St. Francis, also a boarding school, was established in 1885 just seven miles southwest of the Rosebud agency. Within the next decade, day schools cropped up in every district of the reservation. By 1893 six day schools and teachers' residences had been built, and in that year six more were completed. By 1895 the number of day schools on the reservation had increased to twenty-one (Anderson 1971).

Children living in boarding schools during the year were sometimes sent to work as domestics in non-Indian homes during the summer to keep them from their relatives and traditions, a policy that became known as "legalized kidnapping." Because of dire poverty and lack of food, many Lakota depended on free room and board for their children. Free boarding-school facilities were an important factor in luring the Sioux into the schools.

By the 1890s the Lakota were dependent on the government for food, clothing, housing, and the right to use their land. The disintegration of native life had truly begun. There were outbreaks of violence and rebellion. The climate was that of frustration, anxiety, and dissatisfaction. The situation was extremely favorable for the spread of a new religion introduced to the Lakota by the Utes and Paiutes to the west. A new messiah, Wovoka, promised a return to days of prosperity and peace, invulnerability to the white man's bullets, the return of the buffalo, and the ultimate demise of the white man. The Ghost Dance, as the religion was called, was primarily inspired by Christianity, but contained many elements of the native religion—especially dancing until one entered a trance and experienced a vision. In *The Illustrated American,* a newspaper published in 1891, an article appeared describing the reaction to this new religion:

> Both the Sioux and the whites were much excited. The former were ready and willing to throw off forever the odious yoke of oppression; the latter, fearful for the safety of their homes and families. If the dances continued to be religious and there was nothing of a warlike nature introduced, there could be no objection to the Sioux dancing as long and as hard as they desired. But older residents, and those acquainted with Indian warfare, knew well that an outbreak was always preceded by a series of dances. These men . . . failed to discern between a religious ceremony and a war-dance. Hence the very grave error followed of accusing many friendly Indians, who had joined the dance for no other purpose than worship, of hostile intentions.

The whites were sufficiently alarmed to order the arrival of far more troops than were necessary to subdue the dancers. Captain Forsyth of the Seventh Cavalry prepared to disarm the Sioux who had set up their lodges just west of Wounded Knee Creek. Although the Sioux were flying a white flag, their weapons were confiscated; but still one Sioux reportedly fired into a line of soldiers, killing one of them.

> The line of troops replied instantly with a volley . . . killing as many as half the warriors. . . . Women and children attempted to escape by running up the dry ravine, but were pursued and slaughtered . . . there is no other word . . . by hundreds of maddened soldiers, while shells from ten Hotchkiss guns . . . continued to burst among them (Andrist 1964:352).

Approximately three hundred Indians died at Wounded Knee, about two-thirds of them women and children. The Ghost shirts, designed to repel the white man's bullets, proved ineffective, and the Sioux quickly abandoned their faith in the Ghost Dance religion. The 1890 Wounded Knee Massacre thus ended a quarter of a century of political, military, and moral struggle for the Sioux.

It is difficult to assess the effects of these historical events on the contemporary Lakota. In a 1970 study of Rosebud, Ballas states:

> The Dakota have perhaps never completely recovered, culturally or psychologically, from the combined military defeat, loss of the buffalo herds, and the subsequent almost complete dependence on the white man for food and other necessary supplies (1970:33).

This combination of events—the loss of the buffalo and consequent lack of any reliable subsistence base, the breakdown of the native political structure, land allotment, pressures by missionaries and government agents who discouraged and forbade native rituals, and the Wounded Knee Massacre—all contributed to a disintegration of the basic fabric of Lakota life. At the turn of the century, the Lakota were a bitter and demoralized people.

3 / The Rosebud reservation

3.1 THE RESERVATION TODAY

The Sioux are the second largest Native American tribe in the United States (the largest being the Navajo) and reside primarily in South Dakota. In this state, the Indian population comprises 4 to 5 percent of the entire South Dakota population. The South Dakota reservations include: Standing Rock, Cheyenne River, Sisseton, Yankton, Crow Creek, Pine Ridge, and the last two—Lower Brule and Rosebud—which are the homes of most members of the Brule bands.

The Rosebud Reservation, located in south-central South Dakota, is the home of most of the Upper Brule bands of Sioux. The population on the reservation exceeds eight thousand and appears to be increasing steadily. The total official enrollment of the tribe, including those residing in urban (off-reservation) areas, numbers twenty-two thousand. Next to the Brule, the second largest band represented on the reservation is the Oglala, many of whom have intermarried with Brules. Few people identify themselves anymore as Brule or, for that matter, as belonging to any other band. Rather, they consider themselves "Rosebud Sioux," identifying with the reservation community rather than with a particular band. Those who do distinguish between bands recognize only minor differences in language, culture, or attitude with their neighbors, the Oglala.

Until 1977 the reservation was spread across five counties in the state: Todd, with the highest population of Indian people, Mellette, Tripp, Gregory, and Lyman, with the fewest number of Indian residents. As the result of a 1977 Supreme Court decision (*Rosebud Sioux Tribe* v. *Kneip*), the reservation boundary now includes only Todd County. (See Figure 1 to compare current size of the reservation with the larger area indicated in Figure 4.) Total land in the five-county area on the reservation, including tribally owned and allotted land, is 958,200 acres—just under 1 million acres. From its eastern to western boundaries, the reservation spans 135 miles, stretches approximately 60 miles from its northern to southern edges, and includes over 5300 square miles. To the north, the reservation is bordered by the White River; on the south, by the Nebraska state line.

Topographically, the reservation appears as rolling prairie, stark and barren to the eyes of some tourists but beautiful and somewhat awesome to those who know it well. Most of the reservation is grassland. Alternating with the rolling prairie are deep-cut ravines and canyons with large and beautiful stands of ponderosa pine and

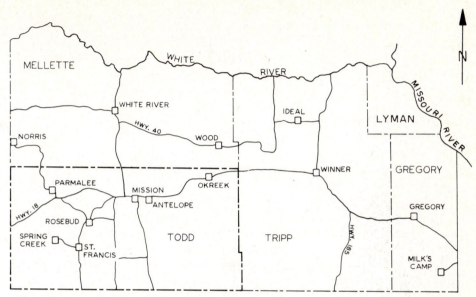

Figure 5. The Rosebud Reservation area (reservation proper is now Todd County only)

cottonwoods along the creeks. These wooded areas are sometimes used as parks and, in the more remote communities, they provide ample habitat for deer. Natural sandhill lakes are scattered throughout the southern reservation area. Some of these, as well as artificial lakes, have been dammed and are maintained for recreational purposes. Wild fruits and vegetables grow and are still harvested all over the reservation, serving as an important supplement to the predominantly western Lakota diet. Chokecherries, buffalo berries, and wild plums are traditional foods that continue to be popular. They are used to make *wožapi,* a berry pudding that is standard fare at every Indian feast. Teas, medicinal roots, wild turnips, and onions still abound and are gathered by those who know how to identify and collect native plants. Those who still know the art dry foods and then braid and decoratively hang them for use throughout the winter months.

The climate in the reservation area is one of seasonal extremes, often causing hardship for its residents. Temperatures in summer commonly reach 105 degrees and not infrequently get as high as 115 degrees. In the winter, temperatures drop below zero part of the time. While precipitation is low (the average is 18 inches per year), and snowfall is not particularly heavy, the wide-open country permits severe drifting during blizzards, often killing livestock and preventing any travel for short periods of time.

Most of the land at Rosebud is grassland and is best suited for ranching. A small portion is irrigated and used for farming. Although some Lakota do farm their own land, most of them prefer cattle-ranching to raising crops, and over half of the reservation—527,800 acres—is used for grazing by Indian ranchers. Aside from the land owned collectively by the tribe, the remainder is leased to non-

TABLE 1.   RESERVATION LAND

527,800 acres	acreage used by Indians
430,400 acres	acreage used by non-Indians
958,200 acres	total reservation land

Indians who do somewhat more farming than the Lakota and nearly as much graz-ing. A total of 430,400 acres of Indian land is leased annually to non-Indians for both enterprises.

Reservation Communities

Most Lakota at Rosebud are settled into twenty communities on the reservation. (See Figure 6.) Of these twenty, most represent native settlements that had been established in the mid-1800s. After the reservation was established in 1868, these villages were listed as original reservation districts, some of which survive today as modern communities with the same names. (See Figure 7.) The original dis-tricts were "camps" composed of bilaterally related extended families. This unit, the *tiyošpaye*, was—and for some communities still is—the basic unit of social life and the "core of Sioux society" (Hassrick 1964:12). The *tiyošpaye* (*ti* means "house" or "dwelling" and *ošpaye* refers to " 'a company separated from the main body,' " Buechel 1970:407,487,491) was the original Lakota community, the group

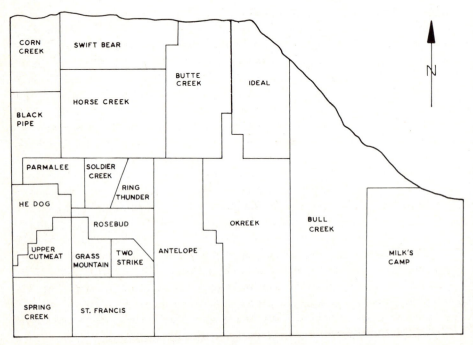

Figure 6. The twenty Rosebud Reservation communities

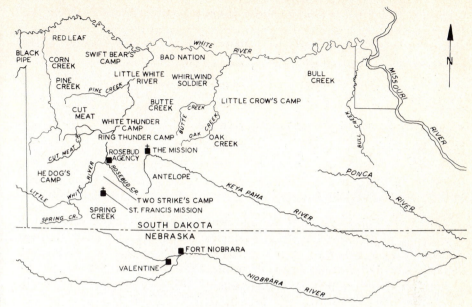

Figure 7. The Rosebud Reservation districts, about 1895

of kinsmen who hunted together. Because the *tiyošpaye* consisted of several related families, marriage was usually outside this group, but within the band. This native community was organized for political purposes under the leadership of a "headman" who exercised judgment and made decisions pertaining to hunting, food distribution, and location of the camp. Although there are no longer community headmen, some of the villages still retain their basic character as a community of related families.

When the Bureau of Indian Affairs began to construct permanent houses for Indian families, the original character of established communities was retained by construction of homes on the original house sites of members of the *tiyošpaye*. Consequently, in the small and rather remote communities, family organization was not radically altered. Today villages such as Black Pipe, Cut Meat, Rosebud, Butte Creek, and Spring Creek are extensions of original *tiyošpaye*. Other communities on the reservation have been newly formed by bringing rural Lakota into housing development project areas. Communities such as St. Francis grew around mission churches that fed and housed many.

The communities range in size from fifty to over twelve hundred individuals. The differences between them are as great as the difference in population size, ranging from the most traditional communities to modern, assimilative ones. They differ in the language that characterizes routine conversation, in unemployment rates, educational levels, and the degree of adherence to native ritual practices. Because of this tremendous diversity, it is impossible to select any one as typical of modern reservation life. For this reason, two communities, Antelope, a native community chosen in the 1960s for a housing cluster development, and Spring

Creek, a community that is a smaller and more regionally isolated *tiyošpaye,* will be compared in depth in the following chapter. Together, they provide a realistic view of the wide range of attitudes, beliefs, and lifestyles that comprise modern Lakota society.

Housing

Within each community, as well as in the more sparsely populated areas on the reservation, housing is provided by the Rosebud Housing Authority through contracts with the federal organization HUD—the Department of Housing and Urban Development. The Housing Authority was established by a tribal ordinance first in 1962 and finally in 1976 in response to an urgent need for decent accommodations:

> There exist on the Rosebud Reservation unsanitary, unsafe and overcrowded dwelling accommodations. . . . There is a shortage of decent . . . dwelling(s) which persons of low income can afford. . . . These conditions cause an increase in and spread of disease and crime and constitute a menace to health, safety, morals and welfare (Rosebud Sioux Tribe Ordinance No. 76-02).

The Housing Authority is controlled by a board of five commissioners, one of whom is appointed board chairman by the Rosebud Sioux Tribal Council. All planning for the contracting, construction, and occupancy of housing developments is subject to the board's approval. Tension and friction frequently develop between the Housing Authority administration and reservation residents, who fear that officials will show favoritism toward their kinsmen and friends.

Most homes built on the reservation are funded and built by HUD, although some housing is built through contracts between the Housing Authority and other corporations, public or private. Depending on the cost of the materials and construction, the Housing Authority establishes the cost of the home and then calculates the tenant's cost based on family income. Some homes are available for purchase and others are strictly rental property.

At Rosebud, most of the houses fall within one of the following types: transitionals, Sioux 400s, low-rent properties, mutual self-help houses, and elderly apartments. Because the contract for each housing project is obtained independently, there is a great deal of variation in the process of becoming a tenant or homeowner. Some houses are purchased through monthly payments over a period of years; others have been given outright by the tribe to the owner at no charge. Because of these differences, there is often animosity about some people having been given their homes while others continue to make mortgage payments. Still others are unable to obtain housing accommodations at all.

Although some Lakota believe that they must have a certain minimum fixed income to qualify for housing, everyone is technically eligible for housing accommodations, even if his or her only income is county or BIA welfare, social security, or disability or unemployment insurance. Even if a person is unemployed, any county, state, or federal assistance is considered "income"; one's projected housing expenses are taken into consideration in determining the rate of support the person is eligible to receive. So although their income may be extremely low, most Lakota can still qualify for housing.

Transitional homes were originally designed and developed by the Battelle Memorial Institute of Columbus, Ohio, to provide homes of limited quality and limited life until alternative housing could be arranged. The Bureau of Indian Affairs, the Public Health Service, the Rosebud Sioux Tribe, and Battelle cooperated in the completion of these homes. The small, two-bedroom houses were constructed at a cost of $5500 each; 375 of them were built, most in established communities and a few on scattered sites where Indian families lived. The houses were to be purchased over a period of five years by the tenant, who paid five dollars a month into a fund established to offset the cost of construction (total cost to the owner was three hundred dollars). At the end of the five-year period, the tenant was to become the owner. Soon after the houses were completed, the Rosebud Sioux Tribal Council commented on their quality:

> These homes were not expected to last for any length of time. . . . It is evident that they may be deteriorating more rapidly than anticipated. Replacements are going to be necessary in the somewhat near future. Despite this deterioration no plans are currently underway for their orderly replacement. Too many Indians view these transitional homes as permanent dwellings. This housing performed a needed function despite their short life—they have filled the transitional gap. The impact of their presence in providing for a more favorable environment for further development cannot be denied (Rosebud Sioux Tribal Council 1971).

Because of the dubious quality of the houses, a year later a tribal policy decision was made to give the houses outright to the prospective owners. Some had made partial payments, some had paid for their houses in full, and others had not paid at all, but the houses became the tenants' property at no additional cost. There is no question that these homes were badly needed and tenants were grateful to get them; however, there is also no question that deep resentment grew among other Lakota who were still obligated to pay for their homes. Resentment was still deeper for those who had not been fortunate enough to have received a house at all. After this transitional contract ended, no additional homes of this type were ever built at Rosebud.

Plans to build a second type of house, the Sioux 400, were drawn up through a contract between HUD, the Public Health Service, and the Bureau of Indian Affairs. Under this "Tri-Agency Agreement," HUD was to furnish the funds for construction of the house, PHS was to furnish the sanitary facilities, and the BIA agreed to furnish the roads. A developer was hired to plan the entire project: two-bedroom homes were built, assembled, and loaded onto trucks and set down on precast foundations. All the tenant had to do was "turn the key" and take occupancy. The houses became known as "turnkey 3" houses and were only locally called the Sioux 400 (because 400 of them were built). Problems with the Sioux 400 homes were great: poor timing among the three contracting agencies resulted in the houses being built and furnished with appliances before the sanitary facilities and drainage had been completed. As a result, the homes were water-damaged and badly vandalized before residents ever moved in. Construction problems were evident also: the heating and ventilation systems were inadequate, doors and windows

The transitional is the smallest of all the house styles on the reservation. All are two-bedroom, Indian-owned properties.

did not function properly, and although tenants were permitted to move in, homes had to be reinsulated, resided, recaulked, and reventilated.

The tribe was once again dissatisfied with the inferior design and construction of the homes and, in a legal settlement, was awarded *all* the Sioux 400 houses at a total cost of a dollar. The tribe, in turn, gave the houses to the tenants free of charge with no mortgage obligations due. Although homeowners had the advantage of a free home, certain disadvantages also accompanied this transaction.

Low-rent housing consists of one- to five-bedroom units. No low-rent units may be purchased—they are the property of the Rosebud Housing Authority.

Since HUD no longer had any legal obligations toward the homes—they had been legally sold and were no longer their responsibility—no provisions were made for insurance or maintenance. Consequently the tenants had to (and still have to) underwrite the cost of home repairs. This is difficult if not impossible for low-income families. The Sioux 400 project did not turn out well for the tribe, and the tribe has no plans to contract for the construction of any more.

Low-rent housing is also contracted through HUD, but is designed to be rental property only; no low-rent units may be purchased. Low-rent housing consists of one- to five-bedroom units built in most of the communities on the reservation. It is an ongoing housing project, and plans for the construction of additional units continue to be made annually. Rent for these units is determined by the Rosebud Housing Authority on a sliding scale and is fixed according to the tenant's income. The fee each tenant pays covers the cost of utilities, maintenance, and renter's insurance. No matter how small an income a family has, the projected cost of housing is, once again, figured into one's state or BIA welfare entitlements, so everyone—regardless of income—is eligible for a low-rent unit.

The mutual self-help homes were originally designed as home ownership properties that were constructed with the projected owner's assistance or "sweat equity." The housing material was brought to the site of construction and ten people built each house. Today, construction is contracted to a builder instead; the mutuals are still designed as ownership properties, however.

Mortgage payments for mutuals are computed on a sliding scale based on the tenant's income (as with the low-rents) and the number of bedrooms. A minimum charge of twenty-five dollars per month is required of each tenant at this time. The contracts for these homes do *not* provide the cost of maintenance, utilities, or repairs—the homeowner must provide them. Because of these expenses, families usually are not eligible to receive a mutual home unless their income is at least six thousand dollars annually. Although the Housing Authority will repair damage from vandalism, it is done at cost to the tenant, so the income level of the family must be high enough to sustain these expenses. Mutuals range from two- to five-bedroom homes, most of which are built in communities, with a few constructed in scattered rural sites. Homeowners are encouraged to put in lawns, shrubs, trees, and fences.

Lastly, the elderly units are one-bedroom rental apartments designed for single individuals or couples over sixty-two years of age, or for handicapped individuals under sixty-two. Once again, rental fees are calculated on a sliding scale. Many elderly people depend on this type of housing accommodation, where arrangements can be made for in-home nursing care.

In addition to new homes, a BIA Housing Improvement Program (HIP) has attempted to alleviate some housing difficulties by providing grants to Indian families living in substandard or inadequate housing to repair existing homes. Some new houses are constructed with HIP funds, but on a very limited scale, and then only to the elderly (people over sixty-two). Housing improvements are made at no cost to the owner. Because it is cost-free, the program is in great demand, and there is usually a long waiting period between the agreement to repair and the actual repair. One of the reasons for the backlog is that funding for HIP—as with so many other programs—has not been sufficient to meet the requests for home repairs (*South Dakota Legal Services Newsletter,* August 1978).

The availability of housing at Rosebud can in no way keep up with the demand. In 1979, there were over 1000 applications for homes. The 1978 housing allocation furnished only 150 homes (low-rents and mutuals), roughly half the number requested. In 1979 the allocation was for only 103—also half the number requested. In 1980, there were still over 800 applicants whose requests were not met; and new applications are continually being submitted. Lakota people who have spent years living and working in urban areas want to return to Rosebud to retire. They apply for housing only to be told that there is a long waiting list. If they decide to apply for a home, the waiting period averages five years. The supply simply cannot keep up with the demand. The housing shortage is critical at Rosebud, resulting in inadequate and overcrowded conditions for many Indian families and, for some, no housing at all. They move in with relatives for years on end. With well under 2000 homes on the reservation and a population of 8000, the housing situation is critical.

Construction of houses is hindered by the complexity of paperwork, as well as by labor problems and a short construction season. It is very difficult to complete all arrangements and construction of an entire housing project within the time allotted. Some families who do not have a house through the Housing Authority live in shacks or log cabins. Lacking central heat, they depend on wood-burning stoves for cooking and heat. In winter this is a severe hardship, because wood is expensive and difficult to obtain.

Although any enrolled member of the Rosebud Sioux Tribe is legally entitled to a home, large families—those with many children or elderly dependents—are given priority. (No blood quantum requirements exist for housing *per se,* but one-quarter Indian blood is required to be an enrolled tribal member.) Lakota who come from the neighboring Pine Ridge Reservation or from other Sioux reservations are legally eligible to apply for homes, but preference is given to enrolled members at Rosebud. Non-Indians are rarely housed unless the Housing Authority feels that the community will benefit by their occupancy.

Many people bitterly complain about their inability to obtain homes. Individuals in their fifties and sixties whose children are grown are less likely to receive a home since they do not have young dependent children; but they are not yet eligible for elderly apartments.

When a family does manage to obtain a house, innumerable difficulties exist regarding maintenance, upkeep, and utilities. Heating fuel, mostly liquid propane, must be purchased in advance and is delivered by truck after prepayment. Although a supply may last for several months, it is difficult for some families to afford the initial cash layout all at once. Many homeowners who are responsible for the upkeep on their houses take great pride in caring for their property. But others cannot pay these maintenance costs and often cannot afford necessary repairs. These homes deteriorate at a rapid rate. Many suffer from total neglect. Some houses have never had running water or indoor plumbing; others have never been hooked up to sewer systems. Where septic tanks are unavailable, outhouses are built by the Housing Authority; but then labor difficulties can result in deep, dangerous pits lying open and unattended for months at a time. Lack of sanitary facilities has serious consequences: for those without access to running water, for example, the lack of regular bathing has resulted in outbreaks of impetigo among children. Although it is easily treated with antibacterial agents, poor hygiene due to the lack of running water persists. Cooking and kitchen chores are more difficult without running water and the level of sanitation becomes miserably low. Although these difficulties are not common throughout the reservation, there are communities where they do exist.

Of all the problems connected with housing, the most serious is vandalism. Because of the high incidence of destruction to property, the Housing Authority does not offer vandalism insurance. Broken windows, disastrous during winter, remain unrepaired until the tenant can afford to fix them. (The Housing Authority will do the repairs, but at the cost to the owner or tenant.) Broken screens and doors result in vulnerability to theft, as well as insect infestation during summer. The lack of repairs gives some reservation communities a rundown appearance, and tenants feel helpless in their inability to pay for all the necessary repairs. Consequently, the situation is left to deteriorate until some houses are abandoned— burned, destroyed, and finally vacated.

Although the housing situation, by any standards, continues to be inadequate to meet the needs of the people, there is no question that it has greatly improved since the early 1960s. Whether changes have been sufficient or adequate remains to be seen. In 1978, a report released by the Government Accounting Office found that "progress in eliminating substandard housing on Indian reservations was slow and that unless the federal government implemented rapid changes, the shortage of houses would increase" (*South Dakota Legal Services Newsletter,* August 1978). The federal agencies that provide housing to Indians—HUD, the Bureau of Indians Affairs, and Farmers Home Administration (FHA)—have been accused of being ineffective in providing the number of units necessary to keep pace with the need. HUD, the largest provider of Indian houses, has been judged too slow in producing houses and has been criticized for not being responsive to Indian needs. Out of a goal of producing six thousand houses annually throughout reservation areas, only three thousand were ever built. Those that are completed are "plagued with defects" (*South Dakota Legal Services Newsletter,* August 1978). The entire program has met with near total failure in eliminating substandard housing among Indian people.

3.2. TRIBAL POLITICAL STRUCTURE

Until 1934, the Lakota had endured several decades of political ambiguity. Their indigenous tribal structure had virtually disintegrated, but had not yet been replaced with a modern system. The adoption of a modern tribal structure began with one of the most important pieces of government legislation ever passed concerning Native Americans: the Indian Reorganization Act (or Wheeler-Howard Act) passed in 1934 under the administration of John Collier, then Commissioner of Indian Affairs. This policy was developed to assist native tribes

in establishing tribal governments and to promote self-rule through the establishment of ongoing economic programs on the reservations. Although the Indian
Reorganization Act was praised as the first major piece of government legislation
to truly benefit Native Americans—it put a stop to allotment of Indian lands—
it has also been criticized for promoting the development of tribal political structures modeled on the U.S. government. Although under the IRA, tribes such as
Rosebud were to have a new form of government, many Indian people believed
that such a government was alien both in structure and purpose to their indigenous
political organization. But in 1935, the Rosebud Sioux Tribe voted to adopt the
provisions of this act, and, in so doing, was issued a corporate charter by the U.S.
Secretary of the Interior. This charter established a representative democracy governed by a tribal constitution and bylaws.

Under this charter, the main governing body of the tribe is the Rosebud Sioux
Tribal Council, consisting of elected officers (president, vice-president, and thirty-
three representatives from the twenty communities on the reservation). In order
to vote in tribal elections or run for office, members of the tribe must be officially
enrolled as members of the Rosebud Sioux Tribe. To be an enrolled member a person must have been listed on the 1935 census roll or must be a descendant of the
original members and must have at least one-fourth or more Rosebud Sioux Indian
blood, regardless of place of residence. (Originally, enrollment in the tribe was
based on blood quantum *and* residence; since 1965, however, there has been no
residence requirement for tribal membership.) Voting privileges are restricted,
though, to those who have lived on the reservation for at least ninety days preceding
the election. Services such as free medical care are available to individuals who have
at least one-eighth Indian blood.

The Tribal Council's functions are to administer programs and services to members of the tribe, to develop and conserve tribal property and resources, and to
regulate all economic affairs of the tribe. In order to carry out these functions, committees are established by the council to deal with programs in such fields as law
enforcement, health, education, and land management.

The committees are governed in a variety of ways, depending on the policy
of the current administration. For example, the Law Enforcement Committee controls the police force of the Rosebud Sioux Tribe. The Health Committee works
with the Indian Health Service in establishing health care services administered to
tribal members. Each program director reports directly to the Tribal Council, which
meets regularly to plan implementation of committee recommendations. In addition
to laying out and implementing the long-range goals of the tribe, tribal programs
are continuously developed that assist Indian people with day-to-day problems. One
such program recently developed is a tribal fund established to pay mortuary
expenses for tribal members. The tribe contracts with mortuaries in nearby off-
reservation towns and arranges for payment of all associated expenses.

Two of the most important functions of the tribe are to protect land held by
tribal members and to purchase land that would otherwise lose its tribal status. In
1943 an organization was formally established within the tribe to deal with problems of fractionated allotments (allotted land that has been divided into fractional

portions). At present the tribe owns and controls over four hundred thousand acres of land, which it leases to Indians and non-Indians for ranching and farming operations. (For a detailed discussion of the Tribal Land Enterprise (TLE), see the section on "The Land" in this chapter.)

In addition to the Tribal Land Enterprise, the tribe operates a Tribal Ranch on nearly forty thousand acres of tribal land. Revenue from cattle-ranching belongs to the tribe and is used to purchase additional livestock and land. Income from the sale of livestock can also be used to pay debts incurred by the tribe.

Relationship with the BIA

The Rosebud Reservation has its tribal headquarters at the agency town of Rosebud and falls under the administrative jurisdiction of the Aberdeen Area Office of the Bureau of Indian Affairs, which in turn is under the jurisdiction of the U.S. Secretary of the Interior. All federal funds are administered to Rosebud (and all other reservations in North and South Dakota) through the director of the Area Office. Although many people believe that the Bureau's control at Rosebud is paternalistic, *most* programs at Rosebud, the majority of which are federal or tribal, are ultimately funded by it. The various departments within the Bureau control such things as the building and maintenance of BIA roads, educational funds, and, most importantly, the sale and leasing of Indian land.

The superintendent of the Rosebud Agency receives his authority through the U.S. Secretary of the Interior, whose function it is to "protect individually owned and tribal lands against waste and to follow rules and regulations under which these lands may be leased or permitted for grazing" as contained in the Code of Federal Regulations (25 CFR, Part 151). Some of the purposes of the regulations are:

(a) to preserve, through proper grazing management, the land, water, forest, forage, wildlife and recreational values on the reservation and improve and build up these resources where they have deteriorated;

(b) to promote use of the range resource by Indians to enable them to earn a living, in whole or in part, through the grazing of their own livestock;

(c) to provide for the administration of grazing privileges in a manner that will yield the highest return consistent with sustained yield land management principles and the fulfillment of the rights and objectives of tribal governing bodies and individual land owners. (*South Dakota Legal Services Newsletter*, October 1978)

The strict control over this major resource results in a classic love-hate relationship between the Lakota and the Bureau. Many Indians deeply resent the heavy-handed control over the sale or leasing of Indian land; on the other hand, they are grateful that care is taken to keep Indian land from being sold to non-Indians. Some of the traditional Lakota maintain that Bureau employees are "sell-outs" (called "Bureau Indians") and that they represent assimilative attitudes and policies as extensions of the government. Yet over half the Indian labor force on the reservation is funded by federal programs. Many Lakota also resent that, through their relationship with the Bureau, the Indian people have gained a reputation as "wards" of the government and recipients of special favors from the government. Yet they also depend on the economic benefits they derive under the Bureau's control—such as not having to pay property taxes on Indian-owned land.

The Land

More than any other single resource, land is what characterizes the unique relationship between the federal government and Indian people; it is the basis for the strong ties and legal obligations that the federal government maintains to Indian people. Although it was the various treaties and acts of Congress that were responsible for reducing the amount of Indian-owned land, it is now a different branch of the federal government—the Bureau of Indian Affairs—that attempts to preserve Indian-owned property and improve the Indian economic situation.

The special trust relationship places Indian people into a set of circumstances that are unique for Native Americans alone; no other ethnic group in America has them. Some regard this relationship as protective and others as debilitating in the dependence it fosters in the Indian people. On the one hand, the government, through the Bureau of Indian Affairs, controls Indian land and prevents its falling into non-Indian ownership by maintaining rigid control over all sale and leasing transactions. The Bureau makes an effort to act in the "best interests" of the individual Indian and the tribe to prevent the alienation of reservation land. (Obvious difficulties arise over what constitutes anyone's best interests.) On the other hand, some believe that the Bureau's exclusive control promotes irresponsibility and prevents Indian economic development through the Bureau's paternalistic approach—so long as the Bureau makes the decisions for Indians regarding Indian land, the Indian people will never learn to manage their own economic affairs and the cycle of dependence will never be broken.

The Trust Relationship: Leasing and Sale

Most reservation land is held in trust for Indian people by the U.S. government and is managed through the Bureau of Indian Affairs. Although any Indian landowner *may* legally obtain the title (technically called "fee patent") to his or her land and own it outright, this option is rarely chosen by the Lakota. Instead, the Lakota prefer that the U.S. government hold all title to Indian land. The United States, then—not the individual allottee—is the *legal* owner as long as the land retains its trust status. This arrangement protects Indian land from sale and taxation. No property taxes are assessed on trust land, and lease income received from trust land is not subject to taxation either. However, people who lease Indian land are assessed a tax on the property. Whether the title is held for an individual allottee or for the tribe, the government (through the bureau) retains control over the land and exercises certain rights over leasing and sale. The rights that constitute trust title include: 1) the right to make final review of any transaction, and 2) the right to approve all transactions. As long as the BIA reserves these rights, no land may be sold or leased without their approval.

Although the government retains legal ownership and control, the Indian allottee (or the tribe, in the case of tribal land) retains rights for the use, occupancy,
and management of the property, subject to the approval of the BIA. Plans for the
use of tribal land must be approved by the Tribal Council as well as the BIA. In
cases where the tribe assigns land to certain individuals or corporations, such as
TLE, the tribe still retains mineral and timber rights and control over right-of-way.

Since all reservation land, whether individually allotted or tribal, is trust land,
leasing and sales are controlled by the agency superintendent, subject to final approval by the Secretary of the Interior. For anyone wishing to lease Indian land,
contractual agreements are drawn up for a three-to-five-year term. Income from
leases is determined according to appraised land values set by the BIA, after which
the Tribal Council sets the minimum rate. Individual owners in Todd and Mellette
County receive a minimum of three dollars per acre for grassland and ten dollars
per acre for farmland. In Tripp, Gregory, and Lyman counties, grassland leases for
four dollars per acre and farmland for seventeen dollars per acre. (Although the
reservation technically includes only Todd County, allotments in the remaining
four counties continue to have trust status.) On tribal land, lease rental rates are
established by the tribe. Because most allotments have multi-ownerships, the superintendent of the agency attempts to consolidate this land into "range units" that
can be used for grazing. In cases where the person wishing to lease the land cannot
make contact with the Indian lessor, the superintendent, in accordance with the
Code of Federal Regulations (25 CFR, Part 151, General Grazing Requirements),
has the legal right, after ninety days, to advertise and ultimately to lease the property without having obtained the Indian's permission. Because of the large numbers of owners of a single allotment, it is often impossible for the superintendent
to locate and make contact with *all* the Indian owners. After the legal waiting
period, the superintendent renews the lease "in the best interests" of the Indian.
Failure to inform the superintendent *not* to lease the land often occurs because the
Indian people are often confused and dismayed by the forms and procedures they
must follow. For Lakota who speak a minimum of English, responding to official
demands is often difficult. But failure to respond gives the superintendent the legal
right to lease the land on behalf of the Indian owner. This act results in great bitterness on the part of the Indians; since they did not authorize the agreement, they
accuse the superintendent (and therefore the BIA) of paternalistic supervision.
When the land *does* get consolidated into a range unit and is leased, the income
any single individual derives from the lease is very low due to continual fractionat-
ing of the allotment. Although the income they receive is tax free, it is so small that
few can live on the small share they receive.

Sale of Indian land is an extremely long and complex process. Great care is taken
to see that sales will serve the best long-range interests of the Indian owner. This
protectorship is part of the trust obligation of the government. An individual
wishing to sell his or her land may do so in two ways: (1) obtain a fee patent and
then sell the land, or (2) enter into a "supervised sale." In the first instance, the
Indian landowner applies to the agency superintendent for a fee patent. The transaction is reviewed and a determination is made as to the advisability of the sale. In
the second case, if the sale is approved, the tribe has a preferential option to buy

the land and retain its trust status. This protects the land from alienation. The tribe has one year to exercise this legal option, and no sale may take place until it releases this option. If the tribe fails to act, the land may be advertised for sale.

Few fee patents are issued on Indian land. If the tribe does not choose to buy the land, the superintendent must decide whether or not the owner is competent to manage his or her own land without any assistance from the Bureau, and obtain an "unrestricted fee title." If the sale is approved, the individual loses all the advantages of trust status. On the day the fee patent is issued, property taxes are due. Only income from sale of the land that is above the appraised price is subject to taxation by the Internal Revenue Service. The disadvantages of outright sale are great, however, which is why so few fee patents are issued on Indian land. They are very difficult to obtain because many Indian people do not have the management training or experience to manage a fee patent without the costly assistance of real estate agents and attorneys.

Because of these difficulties, most landowners wishing to sell their land prefer a "supervised sale" arrangement, which is considered by most to be a safer option. In this type of sale, payment for the sale goes into a trust account for the Indian owner, which he can draw upon at any time. But the land retains its trust status. Neither the sale nor income from the land is taxed. This type of sale has the advantage of providing income for the sale of land to the owner without the disadvantages of taxation or the loss of reservation land.

Land and Economics

Although land is the biggest single economic resource at Rosebud, it remains the most undeveloped. Various difficulties have emerged since the allotment period that prevent such development. One of the provisions of the Allotment Act of 1887 concerned heirship—that is, how land was to be passed on through succeeding generations. Because Indian people did not write wills (and many still do not), property of those who died intestate (without a will) was divided equally among the survivors, according to state law. Over the last century, many allotments have become fractionalized repeatedly to the extent that some 160-acre allotments are owned in common by as many as a hundred people. Two problems result: the first is that shares are too fractional to be suitable for either ranching or farming operations. In such cases the only possible means of developing the land is to merge all the owners' partitions and lease it. This is often impossible, and so the land remains unusable and provides no income whatsoever to its owners. The second resultant problem is that even if the fractionated interests in the allotments were combined to permit economic development, it is nearly impossible to obtain permission from all the heirs to even lease the land. Sometimes the heirs do not agree on what they want to do with their allotments; oftentimes some of them cannot be reached. The result is that, again, no income is derived from the one economic asset the Indian people have.

In instances where allotments *are* large enough to permit a ranching or farming operation, it is difficult for Indian people to obtain loans to establish themselves in

business. The only collateral most Indian people have is land; however, its pro-
tected trust status renders it impossible for repossession—so there is no collateral
available to qualify one for a loan. Ranching requires a large initial capital invest-
ment, which few Indian people can arrange. Getting a start is exceedingly difficult.

Other Economic Activities and Services

Aside from the economic benefits derived from the land, many Lakota seek
employment opportunities in the service agencies on the reservation. A few are
employed in private businesses and education. The opportunities for professional
advancement are limited at Rosebud because so few tribal industries exist. Until
the mid 1970s, several tribal enterprises (in addition to the Tribal Ranch, which
is still in business) provided jobs in companies that manufactured furniture, elec-
trical equipment, and pottery. Today, only the Sioux Pottery industry thrives.

It is difficult for individual Indians to establish businesses because of the collateral needed to obtain loans and because of the lack of management training and
experience that prepares one for beginning a business. The few industries that are
established by the tribe often fail for lack of contracts. The Indian-owned and
-managed businesses that do thrive are generally located in the town of Mission
and include stable community facilities, such as drive-in restaurants, bowling
alleys, barber shops, and jewelry and crafts stores. Loans obtained through the tribe
enable Indians to finance new businesses and are repaid as they become stable.

A few tribal-sponsored programs provide occasional employment in such programs as mortuary services and custom sewing. Funding for elderly women to make
Indian star quilts provides not only supplementary income, but an opportunity for
recreation and visiting. Participants enjoy having work to occupy their time, and
sale of the quilts gives them sufficient funds to purchase additional fabric and supplies. Unfortunately, funding for the quilting program is not stable, and from time
to time the program stops until additional funds are obtained to get it going again.

For those unable to go into business, some employment is available in unskilled
labor (house and road construction), in maintenance and repair of local homes,
businesses, and schools, as law enforcement officers, mechanics, waitresses, janitors,
service station attendants, and as paraprofessionals such as teacher aides and community health workers. Most positions are temporary or tentative and result in a
lack of financial security for many families.

Over half of the work force consists of jobs originating from tribal and federal
programs. The reservation's economy fluctuates as some programs emerge and
others are discontinued for lack of funding. There is little question that there are
simply not enough employment opportunities. The exodus of young people to
urban areas and military service is evidence of this problem. The reputation of
the reservation as having a welfare economy is both the cause and result of necessary dependence on county, state, federal, and tribal services.

At the county and state levels, public assistance is offered to low-income families
in the form of general welfare, Aid to Dependent Children (ADC), State Police,
and the Comprehensive Employment Training Act (CETA). County funds also

provide meals for both Indian and non-Indian elderly ("Meals on Wheels"). For some, this is the only meal of the day on which they can depend. Many Indian people enjoy this opportunity to get together with their friends and socialize.

At the federal level, the Food Stamp Program, a national program instituted by the U.S. Congress under the Food Stamp Act in 1964, helps low-income people buy more food and improve their diets. The program is run under the state's Welfare Department or the Department of Social Services. Eligibility for food stamps is based on income and resources of the household members.

Another federal program that provides food assistance is the Rosebud Sioux Tribe Commodity Foods Program, which supplies low-income families with staple foods on a monthly basis. Funded by the U.S. Department of Agriculture and CETA, this program stems from a contract in which the tribe contributes storage space, pays for the utilities required to maintain it, and is responsible for keeping monthly reports and records of distribution. In exchange, the Department of Agriculture provides dry and canned goods, such as beans, flour, oats, rice, macaroni, canned meats, fruits, vegetables, peanut butter, cheese, dry milk, margarine, and lard. As with the Food Stamp Program, eligibility for this type of public assistance is based on income and resources of household members. One cannot receive both Food Stamps and Commodities in the same month.

Most of the elderly and traditional Lakota rely on Commodities because the supplies are given outright and all they need to do is pick them up monthly. Those who qualify for large amounts of Commodities often share them with families who use Food Stamps. A black market has developed, particularly off the reservation, for the sale of Commodity foods. For instance, a non-Indian in an off-reservation town can purchase five pounds of cheese for five dollars—which supplies the buyer with a bargain and puts five dollars in the Indian's pocket. Such abuses of the program are inevitable and are basically ignored by the authorities. Young Lakota who have small children or more assimilated families generally prefer the Food Stamp Program because it gives them more versatility in menu planning.

In addition to county/state welfare, a federal welfare program known as Supplemental Security Income (SSI) provides emergency income for the blind, disabled, or those with very low incomes. This program, under the Social Security Administration, provides income on a sliding scale based on need. The BIA also has a child welfare program for very poor families with small children.

One of the most important services rendered the Lakota at Rosebud is South Dakota Legal Services, a federally funded, nonprofit corporation organized to provide legal services to low-income people. It deals with problems concerning unemployment, contracts and leases, social security, welfare, dealings with the tribe or BIA, probates, wills, adoptions, guardianships, or consumer problems. Legal Services has offices all over the state of South Dakota and provides assistance to Indians both on and off the reservation. One of their most important functions for the Lakota is community education: pamphlets and newspapers are continually printed to inform Indian people about laws and policies that affect them. Materials are written simply and in a straightforward manner; some are translated into the native language and are broadcast on the radio, which is particularly useful for those

Indian people who do not read English and therefore do not depend on newspapers. Occasionally, workshops are offered to discuss various issues that have been brought to the attention of the public in news articles.

Other programs run by South Dakota Legal Services include the organization of groups to combat domestic violence. One such group is the White Buffalo Calf Women's Society, a statewide women's coalition that deals with the issues of battered women and child abuse, among others. Organizations like these inform Lakota women about where they can get help in their areas, how to work with law enforcement officers, and how to bring attention to their problems. Women receive counseling and, when necessary, are relocated to shelter homes; there they can escape domestic violence and, with sympathetic assistance, consider solutions to their problems.

Federal law enforcement officers are also provided to the tribe since, as a result of the Major Crimes Code, major criminal acts such as homicide, rape, and grand larceny must be handled as federal, not tribal, cases.

Among all basic services provided to the Rosebud Sioux Tribe, the Indian Health Service (a branch of the Public Health Service) is one of the most important. The IHS Hospital at Rosebud, funded by the U.S. Department of Health, Education and Welfare, provides all health services, including a well-baby clinic, emergency and surgery services, maternity care, and all hospitalization needs. Under the provisions of the Hill-Burton Act, Indian people are also eligible to receive free or low-cost health care from hospitals that receive Hill-Burton funds. In addition to IHS care, special medical needs that cannot be met locally are provided through contract health services at IHS expense. Patients are transported to appropriate medical or hospital facilities at no cost to them. For the Lakota at Rosebud, arrangements are usually made for transfer to Rapid City or Denver, depending on the particular need.

The Indian Health Service also provides services other than medical treatment. They cooperate in the installation of sanitary facilities in new homes; they inspect food handlers in public places such as schools and jails; and they work with environmental groups to eliminate conditions that are hazardous to residents' health and safety.

The IHS's policy is to deliver the best possible health care to all the Lakota at Rosebud. This already difficult task is made even more difficult by the fact that traditional Lakota regard the hospital and its staff with deep suspicion and distrust. Many prefer the diagnosis and healing skills of native healers to western medical practitioners and refuse hospital services altogether. Others will accept care and medication, but are reluctant to go to the hospital, where they feel unwelcome. To overcome this problem, a program called CHR—Community Health Representatives—was implemented, in which medical needs are brought to the Indian people at home by local paraprofessionals (CHR workers), who have been trained at the hospital. Medications for such illnesses as diabetes and impetigo are brought by CHR workers to afflicted individuals, eliminating the tensions that accompany hospital visits. The CHR program also provides a source of employment for many Indian women at Rosebud.

As with other federal services provided at Rosebud, the community is critical of, yet dependent upon, hospital services. Complaints about understaffing and a high turnover are chronic. The Indian people feel that interns and medical students serving their residencies at the Rosebud hospital are not yet professional personnel and are forced on them as researchers who need guinea pigs for experiments. Long waits to see available doctors cause inconvenience and resentment, as well as fear of the loss of employment for taking so much time off from work. But complaints aside, the majority of the Indian people rely on and are grateful for the free medical and dental care they receive. Without it, they would be at a tremendous disadvantage, not only because of the formidable cost of medical care, but because of the lack of private physicians within thirty to forty miles of the reservation.

The delivery of free services by the federal government—either through the BIA or not, as in the case of the hospital—has since its inception been a source of great resentment by non-Indians on the reservation, as well as in urban areas. Non-Indian people resent the fact that the U.S. government has placed Native Americans into a special category that entitles them to services at no cost to the recipient, while the non-Indian taxpayer must pay for the same services. Such feelings have resulted in accusations of Indians being "on the dole," "wards of the government," "hang-around-the-fort Indians," and numerous other labels that criticize dependence. The Indian has come to rely on these services not because they are privileged ethnic recipients, but because the responsibilities to provide the services were part of the treaty agreements made when Indian land was relinquished to the U.S. government. A century later this obligation is easily and often dismissed—many non-Indians feel that the government has paid enough for having acquired Indian land. However, since the 1870s, the entire basis of government–Indian relations has been that of providing services and care to cultures unprepared to enter the American twentieth century. The protection of Indian land, the ultimate in services by the U.S. government, is, in fact, only part of the obligation that continues to characterize Indian–government relations. Until Native American tribes can provide all of their own economic resources and services—and perhaps after that as well—the United States must continue to recognize its important obligation to the Lakota and all Native Americans.

4/Two reservation communities

At first glance, reservation towns have a certain character and appearance that makes them seem alike. Similar house types arranged in rows makes one community nearly indistinguishable from the next. But upon spending some time in a particular village, it is not hard to discover that the likeness ends there. From the basic geographic setting to the way children are reared, the communities are fundamentally different. As familiarity with a community increases, one begins to understand that they represent different variations within a culture, perhaps opposite ends of a continuum of cultural adaptation. Each, with its own language and tradition, is the result of a particular set of historical circumstances, and consequently each represents a unique expression of contemporary Indian life. Each has adapted to modern life in its own way, yet is as typical of reservation life as any other. It is this diversity in modern Indian life—rather than a single lifestyle—that is typical of the Lakota today.

In the village of Spring Creek, where over 350 people live, it would not be uncommon to see an elderly woman sitting in front of her home jerking and drying beef as her ancestors did. She might be sitting with her family and talking entirely in the native language, and might not understand English very well, if at all. In Antelope, the largest village on the reservation and the home of nearly 1500 people, a more typical activity might be bowling, playing cards, or having dinner at the local country club. Both villages are Indian. Both are Lakota. Both accurately reflect what contemporary Indian life is like, and it is difficult to say that one is more "Indian" than the other.

The geographic locations of Antelope and Spring Creek account, in part, for the manner in which the two villages were established and for the cultural character they have today. The Antelope community was built as a housing development project in the 1960s through several housing contracts obtained with HUD through the Rosebud Housing Authority (see Housing in Chapter 3). The area selected for the project was a section of flat prairie just one mile east of the town of Mission and directly off State Highway 18, the major east-west route through southern South Dakota. The houses were built in city-block fashion, creating a grid of house lots, complete with driveways, yards or lawns, paved streets, and speed bumps. Today the community resembles a neighborhood in an urban area or a densely populated village. In contrast, the houses constructed in Spring Creek were not built in a city-block grid due to its geographic setting. The old village of

Spring Creek had been established in the lush, hilly, wooded bottomland of the Little White River. The permanently flowing river cut a canyon lined with stands of timber—geographic features that had to be considered in the development of the modern-day housing projects. As a result, each house was built on a site or lot requested by the particular family, some directly on the road, others in the country or far off the road against a backdrop of tree-covered hills. Houses had more space between them, more shelter in the form of bushes and trees, and adjacent undeveloped areas of land that were used for gardens, raising horses, pitching a tipi, or building a sweat lodge. The wild vegetation enabled residents of this village to gather wild fruit, cut wood, and hunt in the fall and winter. Despite the construction of modern homes, the basic character of the village remained. Today, it is a common sight to see children playing and swimming in the river or riding horses down the village roads. Spring Creek has remained relatively isolated because, unlike Antelope, it is located at the road's end—one never passes through Spring Creek en route to some other place. It is ten miles to a grocery store, post office, or service station, seventeen miles to the agency town where all the tribal offices are located, and it is thirty-three miles to the town of Mission, to which people travel weekly for food and supplies, animal feed, laundry facilities, and other needs. Technically, Mission is considered off the reservation and so is the location of other services desired by residents of Spring Creek, such as county welfare.

This first glance at Spring Creek and Antelope shows important differences in the types of communities on the Rosebud reservation. While some are close to town, and consequently close to stores, schools, and jobs, others are remote and isolated, and so have fewer opportunities to take advantage of urban facilities. But the fundamental differences are only in part due to location. It is a century of traditions—their basic cultural character—that has resulted in the enormous differences between them.

Antelope is considered by many to be a progressive or more assimilated community than Spring Creek. The values of Antelope families articulate more with those of the non-Indian society in nearly all realms—jobs, education, language, and basic values. The more traditional communities like Spring Creek seem to express a deeper attachment to the native lifestyle—not a conscious one, but a natural daily life more rooted in the traditional language, culture, and religion.

Antelope

Within the Antelope community, life appears similar to that of any non-Indian town. Children attend school, adults work, and retired or elderly individuals remain at home, often caring for their grandchildren. Even though jobs are difficult to obtain, the unemployment rate in Antelope is quite low. Nearly everyone owns and leases some land, but most Antelope residents derive their basic income from jobs within the tribe, BIA, the nearby Todd County school system, or employment in the business or service of Mission. It is not mere fortune that people from Antelope have jobs—they seek them, train for them, and keep them. It is difficult to say whether the high rate of employment is due to their proximity to Mission or if their attitudes toward working cause them to make maximum use of their location. Most likely it is a combination of the two.

The location only a mile from Mission has brought the Antelope community into close association with the Todd County school system, the largest elementary and secondary school facility in the reservation area. Todd County High School has the reputation of having the highest educational standards of all the reservation schools. It sponsors extensive sports activities for all ages, as well as a variety of programs in the fields of Native American (Lakota) studies. This recently developed program provides instruction in traditional religious practices, native philosophy, Indian history, music, dance, crafts, and native language.

Members of the Antelope community have the highest levels of education on the reservation. The 1973 community education census, shown in Table 2, illustrates the considerable numbers of Lakota who have completed high school or the equivalent (GED), and have finished several years of college or beyond. With over one hundred people with diplomas or two-year college degrees, they are more prepared than most other people at Rosebud for job training, professional development, and full employment.

Most of the homes in Antelope are equipped with electricity, running water, and propane. Nearly everyone has a car or pickup truck, television, and telephone. Everyone shops in town for groceries, rarely depending on native food sources or hunting.

Individuals living at Antelope tend to be of more mixed blood than full blood. Locally they are known as *ieska*, or "half-breed"—literally *ieska* means "interpreter," but it has come to mean "mixed blood" or "breed." At Antelope, Indian people who are full-blooded, or nearly so (three-quarters or seven-eights Lakota), are often labeled as *ieska* also, since their style of life is thought to represent assimilated attitudes. Because Antelope residents tend to be economically more stable than Indians in other communities—they may own or manage local businesses—they are often branded as "breeds" and are looked down upon by traditional Lakota.

Marriage to non-Indians is not infrequent at Antelope. The high degree of intermarriage over the years has had a considerable effect both on the degree to which the native language is spoken and on adherence to traditional kinship roles. In families where one parent is a nonnative speaker, children are addressed in English. With only half the adult population being native speakers, it is not surprising that very few children have any knowledge of the native language at all—and then only in cases where elderly grandparents reside with the nuclear family. Before the housing project was built, the families tended to be extended residential units—three generations under one roof. But crowded housing conditions have generated a need for separate elderly housing, isolating the old from the young and separating those with knowledge of native language and tradition from the young.

This situation is often a source of deep regret for people at Antelope, for they realize that it is becoming easier and easier to lose all ties to the indigenous culture. Young people, unable to communicate with the old—their links to the past—must learn their traditional history, language, and culture in classes taught at the nearby county school, resulting in a rather superficial, or at the very least vicarious, acquaintance with traditional lore. The more inevitable a break with the past appears,

TABLE 2. EDUCATIONAL LEVELS AT ANTELOPE

Years of Education	Ages							Male	Female	Total	Percent of Subtotal
	14–17	18–19	20–25	26–30	31–40	41–60	61+				
1–8	34	3	4	4	11	42	31	70	59	129	22
9–11	66	15	28	20	27	45	17	103	115	218	37
12	2	22	41	19	22	30	4	74	66	140	24
GED	—	1	6	2	—	6	—	4	11	15	2
13–14	—	4	16	12	14	10	3	27	32	59	10
15+	—	—	10	7	7	4	2	17	13	30	5
Subtotal								295	296	591	100
Unknown										90	
Total										681	

the more involved the community becomes with the school's efforts to provide knowledge of these subjects.

Young people from Antelope depend heavily on the town of Mission for recreation and entertainment. Ball games during all seasons bring young people together during tournaments and school sports competition, providing the major recreational outlet for school-age young adults. The only remaining recreational facilities, all located in Mission, include a bowling alley and café, two drive-in restaurants, and one movie theater. The lack of additional recreational facilities is often cited as the reason young people drop out of school and join the military service: they are bored and restless. Still worse, many believe it is the fundamental cause of heavy involvement with alcohol and drugs.

Spring Creek

Aside from the radically different geographic setting, the most striking thing one notices upon a first visit to Spring Creek is the large number of people at home. Although some adults do venture away from the village daily to go to work, the unemployment rate is very high. While it is true that jobs are scarce, this community appears to participate even less in the western economy than Antelope residents because working outside the home is a somewhat more alien idea than it is at Antelope. Being more oriented toward the routines of traditional life, few individuals seek the income reliability or job security of the white middle class. The majority of employed people tend to have the kind of jobs that enable them to remain close to home, such as in road construction, driving a school bus, or doing janitorial work in the day (elementary) school. At present, little is being done to increase the economic opportunities for Spring Creek residents. In those families where parents are away at work, children are cared for—and raised, really—by their grandparents. This has tremendous influence on the children, because in this community, the elderly are not housed separately: they either live with or near their children, more similar to the traditional pattern.

A number of families in Spring Creek live in homes without running water and indoor plumbing. Nearly all homes are equipped with electricity, though some families do not have all the modern appliances. Those without refrigerators have the problem of food spoiling quickly; worse yet, many families have so little income that they cannot afford perishable items such as meat, dairy products, or fresh produce. Those who dry and jerk meat fare rather well, although children often do not receive adequate amounts of fresh food. The canned and dried goods provided by the Commodity Foods Program supplies the necessary nutrients for minimal health, but the diet is basic and simple, and is built around foods high in starch, such as beans, rice, macaroni, oatmeal, and flour. The starchy diet contributes to obesity, especially harmful in a population already suffering from diabetes. The lack of running water is an inconvenience many Lakota have learned to live with. Teenagers have access to dormitory showers at the boarding schools in nearby St. Francis, as well as in Mission, during the school year. But babies, children, and adults have to make the best of the situation by using—by the bucket—water brought and stored in tanks. The spread of skin diseases such as impetigo remains unchecked in small children and is virtually untreatable without constant washing. Children frequently have open sores and scabs that appear never to heal.

For most children, the early years are spent with their grandparents, who speak to them almost exclusively in the native language. Although their parents may speak to them in English, the children are already native speakers from being raised by their grandparents. The entire community, then, speaks Lakota. Another reason for the survival of the native language is the fact that as an indigenous community, there are few mixed bloods (*ieska*) and *no* non-Indians. Although a few people are married to non-Lakota Indians (such as Apache), there are no non-Indian spouses.

Living a more traditional lifestyle, children are not forced into the non-Indian models of behavior. Although they are avid ball players—basketball in the winter and softball in the summer—they also enjoy the freedom and recreation of a more rural life—riding ponies, picking chokecherries, and swimming in the river. Although the children must attend school, as they do in any other community, the forces that shape their lives while not in school are more the activities engaged in by the adults in their lives—not the western-type activities as in Antelope, but the concerns of a more traditional, rural life. Children frequently help their parents care for livestock or chickens; they repair fences, feed horses, or help construct a sweatlodge for a healing ceremony planned by a community member. Especially important in learning the indigenous culture, children are brought along to native rituals—even those held through the night—observing and absorbing native traditions between naps. Their goals become those of their parents, and the means to achieve them is similar as well. Their continuous exposure to all facets of native life provides them with an intimate knowledge of their traditional culture—information unavailable to children whose parents no longer participate in native affairs. From the time they are born, children attend native rituals, speak Lakota, and learn native music; they watch the preparation of native foods, including *wožapi,* a berry pudding, *wasna,* a pemmican made of dried beef, fruit, and fat, *taniga,* a soup made of cow intestine and considered a delicacy, boiled dog, wild turnips, and other foods rarely tasted by children in other communities. Boys watch and learn how to butcher and skin animals, and girls still learn how to jerk meat and cook food the traditional way.

Without question, it is the intense exposure Spring Creek children have to native life that equips them with knowledge of the indigenous culture—a situation impossible for children in a community like Antelope. Learning traditional values is also an automatic part of daily life in Spring Creek, for the behavior of the old people is still very much in keeping with the native style.

But life lived in this traditional style also has its price. Children are somewhat less prepared—both in concept and in practice—for employment and economic self-sufficiency in the surrounding non-Indian world than are children from Antelope. School is a more foreign experience, and, living a more traditional lifestyle, they are often unable to integrate the substance of their public school education into their daily lives. The lack of meaning that public schooling has for people at Spring Creek is reflected in the low education levels, shown in Table 3. The 1973 community census showed that most of the residents had completed only grade

TABLE 3.   EDUCATIONAL LEVELS AT SPRING CREEK

Years of Education	Ages							Male	Female	Total	Percent of Subtotal
	14-17	18-19	20-25	26-30	31-40	41-60	61+				
1-8	10	2	4	6	12	24	9	36	31	67	46
9-11	12	5	10	8	7	8	—	22	28	50	35
12	—	2	12	4	6	—	—	12	12	24	17
GED	—	—	1	—	1	—	—	1	1	2	1
13-14	—	—	1	—	—	—	—	—	1	1	1
15+	—	—	—	—	—	—	—	—	—	—	—
Subtotal								71	73	144	100
Unknown										23	
Total										167	

eight; twenty-four had completed a high school education, and only three had had any schooling beyond the high school level. Although adults want training and education for their children and encourage them to obtain the skills necessary for potential employment, most of the schooling meets the needs of literacy but falls short of preparing them for work in the non-Indian society. Due to problems of language and cultural conflict, educational standards often are not on a par with other state schools in urban areas. Relaxing of standards, once considered a favor to Indians in the multiethnic classroom, has for some resulted in an inability to compete with non-Indian students from other school systems.

Sharing a different set of values and priorities, school remains an isolated experience for most children in a community such as Spring Creek. Many do not finish high school but drop out as soon as they are legally of age (sixteen), only to find that they are ineligible for the already scarce jobs. Often they leave the reservation in search of job training. Young adults who do not either join the military service or leave Rosebud under programs such as the Job Corps for training find themselves bored, restless, and looking for excitement. The result, all too often, is the deadly combination of alcohol, drugs, and cars. Alcoholism is a disease that plagues young and old alike. Along with traditional patterns of culture that children learn, they learn about alcoholic sprees, drunken binges on payday, and the physical violence that all too often accompanies heavy drinking.

Modern Life at Rosebud

Using these two communities as illustrations of the diversity in reservation culture, it becomes evident that there are many different styles of Indian life. The traditional anthropological model of "traditional" culture as opposed to "assimilated" or "acculturated" really does not accurately reflect Indian life today. Most indigenous tradition, including native language, has undergone considerable change during the last hundred years. Labeling what existed a century ago as "Indian" and calling Indian life today "assimilated" implies that today's Lakota are not Indian, which is not the case. Lakota society today *does* reflect westernization—adaptation to an entirely new economy, adoption of a new technology, absorption of new values, and borrowing a new language. But the manner in which all these elements have converged with the indigenous patterns has resulted in a modern reservation culture that is not at all uniform, but reflects the real heterogeneity that depends on the individuals, historical circumstances, geography, political situation, federal government, and every other possible influence on Indian life.

The Lakota who enjoy ball games *and* powwows, sweat lodge ceremonies *and* bowling are Indians whose lives have adjusted to new circumstances, but whose underlying frameworks and value structures are Lakota. To the non-Indian, these elements are paradoxical and cannot mesh; for the modern Lakota, they *are,* and in *their* lifetime always have been, meshed. Those people on and off the reservation who accept this new blend capitalize on it. Sale of commercial items such as machine-made blankets with Indian designs and modern jewelry with Indian geometric patterns all reflect the new discovery: Indian life is modern, but it is still Indian. Indian people need blankets, but they prefer them with Indian designs, because that is less of a departure from the native concepts of beauty. Institutions such as the church also capitalize on the new culture: the sacred pipe is used as part of the Christian church service, the altar cloths have beadwork on them, the prayer-books and sermons are in Lakota.

A certain incongruity may exist for the outsider, but for the Lakota of Rose-bud, *this* is tradition. Being "Indian" does *not* mean never using the IHS hospital. Having a full-time job does *not* mean never attending a healing ceremony. Raising your children to speak English does *not* mean that you have no knowledge of tra-ditional values. Participating in the Sun Dance does *not* mean that you don't buy your groceries in the supermarket.

The ways in which Lakota and non-Indian cultures are merged are infinite, and have produced a reservation culture in which, on the one hand, people may adhere to a lifestyle similar to one lived at the turn of the century. On the other hand, Indian elements may be nearly or totally absent. One of the areas in which Lakota and non-Indian elements have been uniquely merged is in religious practices. Despite the continuing popularity of native religion, the incorporation of Chris-tianity into nearly all aspects of modern life serves as a clear example of the new blend of these seemingly disparate elements. (See Chapter 6 for a detailed dis-cussion of this topic.)

5/Community life

The routines of daily life on a reservation are no different from life anywhere else: children go to school, adults work, and family life provides the structure within which these routine activities take place. But for the Lakota at Rosebud, much of the activity revolves around traditional social events that constitute the heart of reservation life and make life at Rosebud distinct from the non-Indian society.

Similar to most other reservations in the Plains area, two social events occur with great regularity that have come to characterize modern Indian life: the *powwow* and the *Giveaway*. Although elements of both are considered sacred, they are really social events and the only community affairs other than traditional rituals that provide public recreation. Both the powwow and Giveaway have their roots in the traditional culture and, over the years, have come to incorporate many elements of the non-Indian society. Both have come to symbolize modern Indian identity, and, for those who no longer participate in native rituals, they are the major activities that distinguish reservation life from non-Indian urban or rural American culture.

Both the powwow and Giveaway are tied to native life since their celebration requires a knowledge of Lakota music and dance, traditional dress, custom, and procedure. For some, attending these affairs may be the only opportunity to hear the native language spoken or listen to speeches made by the more traditional elderly. For the young, these activities may be strictly social, an opportunity to meet and socialize with one's friends; for others, it is an opportunity to receive free food, earn money from the sale of food items in concession stands, or merely pass the time. Powwows and Giveaways occur with such regularity that they constitute the main recreational activities for all the reservation's residents. All year round, posters advertise powwow celebrations to such a degree that it seems that people reckon time from one powwow to the next.

The Powwow

The contemporary powwow is an outgrowth of traditional singing, drumming, and dancing, some of which is strictly Lakota in origin, but most of which is the result of over a century of exchange with other Plains tribes. The Lakota call the powwow *wačipi* ("they dance"), but it is considered more than just a tribal function.

For the Lakota, powwows are believed to have originated with the Lakota Grass Dance Society, which learned various styles of dance from the Ponca, Omaha, and Pawnee tribes during the eighteenth century. Regardless of their specific tribal origin, knowledge of the different types of dances is common throughout the reservation, all throughout the Plains area, and even beyond, extending to all parts of the United States. Today Indian dance has come to represent an expression of Indian identity. The powwow provides the opportunity for young and old to don native dress and express "Indianness" in a manner that is considered socially acceptable. It is an event during which it is considered acceptable—even prestigious—to be an Indian. Although the Lakota, like other tribes, are supremely conscious of their individual tribal heritage and identity, the powwow brings together Indian people to celebrate the unity that such an Indian event expresses.

Powwow celebrations are basically Indian social dances at which groups of drummers and singers provide musical accompaniment to a variety of dances. In recent years, contests have developed and young people compete, often for prize money. Panels of judges choose winners based on the appearance of the dance outfit (for men, this might include a feather bustle, head ornaments, arm and leg bands; for women, shawls, leggings, and mocassins); the quality in manufacture (whether any parts of the outfit fall off during the dance); and the ability to dance in perfect time with the drum, without making errors. Many young people enjoy the competitive aspects of the powwow and look forward to traveling throughout the Plains to enter and compete in the powwows held in their or a neighboring state. The family often accompanies the contestant, camping and visiting relatives in the vicinity.

Powwows vary in kind and in size: the local powwow is an intimate, social affair sponsored by one particular community on the reservation, such as Spring Creek, Antelope, or Ring Thunder. Such powwows might be held as a holiday celebration on nonnative occasions such as the Fourth of July, Thanksgiving, or Veterans Day. Although they are open to the entire reservation, the event is localized, with most people coming from the immediate vicinity. These powwows seldom have dance contests in which dancers compete for purses or prizes; rather, they are strictly social affairs and are intended for everyone's enjoyment.

Large tribal powwows occur throughout the year, but mostly during the summer. Although people may come from other reservations, it is primarily a reservation affair, and is usually associated with an annual fair, rodeo, or Sun Dance. The Annual Rosebud Fair, which takes place at the end of summer and symbolically closes the local powwow season, is an event that most Lakota greatly look forward to, and large purses are offered for winners in the dance competition. Dancers who win at these powwows go on to compete in the elaborate intertribal powwows. Concession stands are set up around the outside of the dance area in which food, jewelry, and Indian clothing are sold. The walkway provides young people with a chance to see their friends and socialize.

Most dramatic and exciting of all the powwows are the huge intertribal festivities, which take place throughout the northern and southern Plains and beyond, either on reservations or in urban areas. Powwows such as Crow Fair, the Gallup Inter-Tribal Indian Ceremonial, and those in such places as Bismarck, Tulsa, and

Denver attract Native Americans not only from the Plains states but from every corner of the United States. These affairs provide an opportunity for unity among Native American tribes, which is rarely expressed in other ways. People from different tribes enjoy seeing the dance outfits typical of each tribal group and, armed with tape recorders, they learn the tribal songs performed by each group. Large purses offer incentives for dance competitions, which take place in the afternoons and evenings for three or four days. At the final dance of the weekend, winners are awarded their prizes. At these intertribal events, it is common to see hundreds of tipis and tents erected for weekend camping. Motels are jammed, people wander around on horseback, and parades, fairs, and rodeos are scheduled throughout the weekend. Many Indian people travel the "powwow circuit" all summer long, journeying from reservation to reservation to observe and participate in these spectacular festivities. Visitors from different reservations are often publicly welcomed and are, upon occasion, honored with gifts. Owners of cars with license plates from different states are frequently asked to stand and be acknowledged; when possible, contributions are collected to help offset the cost of their travel. This unity and mutual aid among members of different tribal groups creates an atmosphere of political harmony and social integration.

Most of the people who attend powwows do so because they provide recreation and entertainment. Spectators enjoy the drama and excitement of the music and drum combined with flamboyant and brilliant outfits. Unlike a performance in which the majority are merely spectators, nearly everyone participates, even those who do not bring or wear elaborate outfits. Men generally don special powwow dance outfits, although singers and others may occasionally dance without any special attire. Women may wear elaborate outfits, but for them only a shawl is necessary. Both young and old spend a considerable amount of time fashioning their powwow outfits, which must be made with care and precision so that no parts of the attire fall off during the dance. The opportunity to learn about native dance clothing provides the stimulus for the old to teach—and the young to learn— about the native birds and animals whose pelts and feathers once provided the only ornamentation available. Now, most of the items used in making dance outfits

Crow country is considered the "tipi capital" of the world, especially during the intertribal Crow Fair.

are commercially manufactured, especially necessary since use of eagle feathers for making the outfits had been outlawed by environmental conservation laws. Today, use of eagle feathers is permitted by passage of the Indian Religious Freedom Act. Under this law, Native Americans may hunt birds or purchase feathers to be used for ceremonial purposes. Beads, hair pipes (now made of plastic but once fashioned from bone), eagle and turkey feathers, and cloth are used in creating the costumes, and often represent intricate and painstaking work. The dancer who emerges in full powwow regalia is a truly spectacular sight. Although supposedly the outfit represents traditional dress, most often the appearance is—as with everything else—a unique combination of native and western elements.

Various types of dances comprise the basic repertoire at even the simplest pow-wows. The main styles include: straight or traditional dancing, fancy dancing, and round dancing. Generally it is the first two types that are performed in contests, the third being more a social dance style. Dancers are segregated by sex for judging, so competitions occur within each category of dancers. Each dancer is judged for the specific contest he or she has entered. The criteria vary for each category (for example, men's traditional or girl's fancy dance), but all dancers are judged

Men's traditional dance outfits are beautiful and sedate and are made largely of natural materials.

Women often design and make their own shawls. Many prefer to use traditional symbols in their needlework.

on the quality of their clothing, their ability to keep time with the music, and their ability to dance properly in the style they have chosen.

Powwows combine the excitement of dance competition with social dances in which all people participate, regardless of age or sex. An announcer, or "M.C.," in association with the powwow committee, designates the nature of the dance competitions, social dances, and any other events to be held during the weekend powwow celebration, such as a Giveaway. The announcer designates which drumming and singing group is to perform each song, each taking a turn.

Nearly everyone on the reservation attends the powwows—if not to participate, then to observe. Many families bring tents and spend the entire weekend on the powwow grounds. They either bring picnic supplies or purchase food at the concession stands. Elaborate displays of locally manufactured Indian beadwork, women's shawls, and jewelry are offered to Indians (and non-Indians) visiting from other areas; this exchange often results in the borrowing of designs and styles, and inspiration for local artists. Occasionally local Indian artwork is publicly displayed and sold to the highest bidder. In addition, shawls, blankets, and attractive dance outfits are sometimes raffled off.

The powwow is the primary locus of the real exchange or borrowing of the tribal traditions throughout the Plains. Dancers learn the movements of neighboring tribes' dances, songs are exchanged by the regional drumming groups, and local costuming ideas flow across tribal boundaries. The powwow is a general celebra-

People of all ages enjoy the quick and exciting music and dancing of the powwow.

Women's traditional dress uses native elements such as buckskin and bone.

tion of Plains life—and the best opportunity today for a public declaration of Indian identity. The traditional people enjoy the native elements; the modern Native American takes the opportunity to explore his own "Indianness." And the spectators enjoy being bedazzled by the brilliant crowd of thousands of Indian people from dozens of tribes . . . all, at least temporarily, unified.

Although most Lakota relish the opportunity to attend powwows, there is a small segment of the population that does not participate because they fear any adverse effects they or their children might suffer. Two types of situations occur at powwows that are specifically avoided: coming into contact with drunken individuals who are likely to become involved in fights, and possible confrontation with members of the American Indian Movement.

Although alcohol is technically forbidden anywhere at Rosebud (and on the reservation), its availability in towns adjacent to reservations such as Mission, makes purchase easy. Young people who often drink heavily on the weekends are likely to either drink before they arrive or sit in cars and drink at the powwow. The likelihood of fights erupting is greatly increased under the influence of alcohol, and physical violence, while not a regular occurrence, does happen. Serious arguments result in an occasional fistfight or, worse, a stabbing. The memory of these events deters some from attending powwows no matter how appealing the music and dance might be.

Few powwows become arenas for political debates or encounters between AIM members and the law. However, many conservative Lakota at Rosebud fear these occasional disturbances, and so stay away from powwows and any potential encounters. In the years since the 1973 occupation of Wounded Knee, several incidents on the Rosebud Reservation have turned many Lakota against AIM, if only in fear of their violent tactics.

The last group on the reservation to avoid powwows are those who believe that celebrations of native song and dance are only ties to a past that is better forgotten. Most often these are Lakota who have had bitter experiences in boarding schools or who have felt economically disadvantaged because of the lack of a competitive education. They feel that modern expressions of "Indianness" are shallow substitutes for a native lifestyle that they were forced to relinquish. Any continuing associations with indigenous tradition are only regarded as things that will keep their children from gaining the expertise they need to compete in white society. They believe that the old ways are better forgotten. For them, participation in affairs such as the powwow dooms their children to forever being outcast in the dominant society. They see such participation as going "back to the blanket," and they believe such activities are irrelevant to modern life.

Most Lakota attend and enjoy powwows; those who do not frequent them are the exception, and they usually cite one of the above reasons. But for the majority, powwows are a welcome social activity, an engrossing weekend that combines traditional music, dance, food, speeches, and, most of all, the freedom to be Indian. The great distances traveled are evidence of the powwow's popularity. Some keep their cars supplied for the occasion: lawn chairs or blankets and a set of plastic or aluminum dishes are always ready to go. The amount of time, energy, and money put into dance costumes also illustrates the engrossing popularity of the powwow; for some, preparation of native costumes is a hobby. For those who make shawls, bustles, breast plates, and beaded and quilled items, it is the only way they know to make a living.

Although the tribe does not officially feed those in attendance, rarely is there a powwow in which there is no feast. The host is generally the sponsor of a Giveaway ceremony, part of which is a meal provided to everyone attending the powwow.

The Giveaway

Although many Giveaways are held separately from the powwow, Giveaways have come to be associated with powwows because the latter provides a public event that virtually guarantees a large number of Lakota in attendance. The Giveaway, once a strictly traditional and serious ritual event, has become, under some circumstances, a secular event that takes place within the framework of the powwow.

Originally the Giveaway was a ceremonial distribution of goods that marked the end of the period of mourning (one year) for a deceased individual. The year-long period was part of the observation of the Keeping of the Soul ceremony, one of the seven sacred rites of the Lakota. (See Chapter 6 for a discussion of this ceremony.) Although Giveaways once were held exclusively to terminate this mourning period—and subsequently to commemorate the anniversary of the death each year—the Giveaway has evolved into a more generalized, all-purpose social event, not only at Rosebud, but throughout the Plains region. It is a tradition that embraces the native values of reciprocity and sharing, and one that has become increasingly important for many reservation communities today.

The Lakota call the Giveaway *wiȟpea* (from *wiȟpeapi,* "they give away"), a term that refers to a general public distribution of goods. In the late 1800s—as well as today—Giveaways were held primarily to honor an individual; when someone returned safely from battle, military service, or war, for instance, this was a way of showing gratitude for the person's safe return. In recent years the ceremonial celebration has become the most appropriate means of acknowledging nearly every type of event on the reservation, but has retained its primary characteristic as a vehicle for thanking or giving something back to a community that has provided assistance or support. Today a Giveaway might be held to honor a young woman elected homecoming queen; to express a candidate's gratitude for political election; to honor a birth, marriage, or graduation; to honor an individual who has performed an impressive deed; or simply to express that one is moving on in years and no longer has any young dependents. Giveaways are held for every conceivable reason, and it is not uncommon for a person to stage a Giveaway simply because the family feels it should, as a way of expressing gratitude and affection for one's friends.

Gift-giving has always been a traditional means of establishing family status and gaining prestige. During the late 1800s, distribution of goods rendered people materially poor but raised their status through the display of generosity. Not only was gift-giving a means of equalizing status by preventing a family from acquiring too much property but it also prevented the accumulation of goods that were difficult to transport.

Horses, ponies and buffalo robes were common gifts, and today have been replaced with quilts, shawls, and household items. Occasionally a family still gives away a horse but the great expense generally precludes this. Gifts given never represented true economic specialization wherein a family which produced one type of item traded with another family which produced a different one. If similar objects were traded, the purpose of the exchange had to be for reasons other than the accumulation of goods. Giving was not motivated by purely "economic" reasons as much as it was *socially* motivated. Naturally, families made use of the gifts they received, and still do, but the point of the gift was its meaning—the generosity it expressed and the relationship it symbolized. This basic value of generosity and sharing—*waćanthognaka* in the native language—has remained in Lakota society; prestige and security is still awarded to families who make it a point to give generously to their friends and neighbors. By the same token, families who derive public benefit from but do not occasionally stage Giveaways themselves are criticized for their greed. Social pressure usually compels a family that is moving upward financially to sponsor an elaborate Giveaway, thereby returning to the community the support that the family received and that enabled it to thrive. Such social pressure once may have prevented an uneven accumulation of wealth or a stockpiling of goods. But more importantly, a family's success is always attributed, at least in part, to community support. Unless the community is properly thanked and, at least symbolically, reimbursed the family's status will decline. Once the support of friends in the community has been publicly acknowledged with gifts, the family's good name and generous character are reinstated.

Considering the low income of most Lakota, it is surprising to the outsider that so many people stage elaborate Giveaways and feasts, for the event usually costs several hundreds, or even thousands, of dollars. Although this represents a financial hardship for the sponsoring family, the payoffs far outweigh the disadvantage of temporary material poverty, for those who give generously throughout their lives not only earn the respect of the community, but gain the assurance that they will be taken care of or will have friends to turn to at some later time of need. This is not to say that Lakota only give in order to make their own futures more secure. They give because honoring with gifts is a long-standing cultural tradition.

More than any other event, it is the Giveaway ceremony in which the Lakota philosophy is put into practice. Gifts are seldom given to one's kinsmen, for the purpose of giving is to insure a strong bond between the giver and the recipient, a bond that is already secure among kinsmen. Gift-giving insures that a bond will be newly created, for the recipient must, at some future time, return a gift in kind or a favor. The continual establishment of bonds draws people into a web of reciprocal obligations that fosters mutual aid and care, which is especially important during difficult times. The network of mutual support is often cited as the reason so few Indians carry insurance. They feel that the relationships they have established insure them of help when necessary and that this bond offsets the need for the monetary security that commercial insurance provides.

Most Giveaways begin with an honoring song, as the sponsoring family dances around the goods set out for distribution.

The elaborate display of goods shows the generosity of the family at this memorial Giveaway.

This philosophy, expressed by some informants as "what goes around comes back around," provides comfort and security, particularly to those who have given graciously over the years. The continual cycle of reciprocal exchange has come to underlie all other Lakota values; generosity, above all other virtues, is considered the single most important character attribute. The Lakota have an expression, sometimes sung—*tokša ake luha,* "you will have it again"—that sums up their view of the world: you reap only what you sow, and, ultimately, you will fare in life only as well as you have done for others.

Once a family has decided to stage a Giveaway, numerous arrangements must be made. Depending on whether the ceremony is a mourning ceremony (*wašigala*) or an honoring Giveaway, different arrangements will be made. In both cases, the gifts themselves must be made or purchased. Women begin sewing and hire others to make quilts or to quilt tops for them. In the case of a memorial Giveaway, the need for making arrangements brings the family together with friends, providing much needed support during the period immediately following the loss. Shopping for gift items to be given is a continual process: towels, bedding, yard goods, dishes, trunks, pots and pans, and other assorted kitchen paraphernalia are purchased and reserved for distribution. Quilts and shawls that one has received in Giveaways are rarely regiven; however, commercially made or packaged goods may be reserved and redistributed at one's own Giveaway. Often, relatives (who do not receive gifts) help the sponsoring family accumulate gift items for distribution by contributing packaged goods that they had once received.

In addition to arrangements for the gift items, an announcer must be commissioned to oversee the actual event, and priests, ministers, and/or medicine men are requested to offer prayers on behalf of the individual being honored. Food preparation involves ordering bakery goods, the purchase of a cow or pig, arrangements for butchering and cooking the meat; the women divide up the labor of cooking the remainder of the food to be served.

The Giveaway ceremony usually begins with the singing of the Sioux National Anthem, particularly when the Giveaway is part of a powwow. If the family is honoring a veteran, or if the event takes place on a patriotic holiday, American

A feast is an important part of every Giveaway. Beef or pork is usually the main course. (photograph courtesy of James A. Gibson)

flags are also raised and honored. After the announcer delivers a speech explaining the reason for the Giveaway, the singers and drummers play an honoring song, for which all spectators stand in respect. The announcer, continually conferring with the sponsor, calls each recipient up to receive his or her gift. Gifts are intended for specific individuals who have been most helpful or supportive to the sponsoring family. For instance, during a commemorative Giveaway, gifts of star quilts or shawls are made to friends who assisted the mourning family during the initial period of hardship immediately following the death. Gifts are given to those who remained all night at the wake, or to those who were particularly generous in feeding or caring for the grieving family. Often, money is given to friends and occasionally the sponsor will remove a personal item of jewelry he or she is wearing and place it around the neck of an especially cherished friend.

The Lakota do not verbally respond to the receipt of gifts, but accept the gift with humility and grace. No thanks are necessary. The recipient shakes the hand of the donor or the hand of the individual being honored, and quietly returns to his or her seat, leaving the gift folded and wrapped. Later at home it will be opened.

Following the distribution of gifts, speeches are delivered by the men who have been selected for that purpose. In the case of a memorial Giveaway, their eulogies are followed by a brief period of public mourning at which Lakota women openly weep. Occasionally—such as at a Giveaway celebrating a marriage—an elderly woman delivers a speech dealing with such topics as the importance of raising a family properly. These speeches are considered moral lessons for young people: they are not only spoken in eloquent Lakota by fine orators, but are considered part of the traditional imparting of wisdom by respected elders to the young. Speeches like this are often followed by trills of victory or approval by the women. A drum beat or comments by men officially mark the end of the speech.

After the distribution of gifts is complete, a feast is provided for all those in attendance. The meal usually includes boiled beef or pork, an assortment of salads, breads, and crackers (including Indian fry-bread, *wožapi* (berry pudding), bakery or locally prepared cakes, and coffee. Sometimes very traditional foods such as *wasna* (pemmican, dried jerked beef mixed with fat and fruit) and *taniǧa* (soup made from the intestine of the buffalo or cow) are served, considered great delicacies by the more traditional. Everyone is encouraged to eat their fill and take home whatever food remains for their families. Plastic containers are usually brought for this purpose.

When the meal is finished, spectators quietly drift away, or when the Giveaway is to be followed by powwow dancing, preparations begin for the festivities. (For additional information on the Giveaway, see Grobsmith 1979a.)

Besides the powwow and the Giveaway there are various other occasions that may also have originated in native ritual but, like the Giveaway, have evolved into personal and community affairs. Some events are traditional; others are Indian versions or interpretations of western activities. Regardless of their origins, they have come to characterize modern Indian life.

A number of these occasions revolve around rites of passage or life-crisis rituals that signal the passage of a person from one social group into another. The birth of a baby is celebrated—as everywhere else—as a joy and blessing to the family. Today, some Indian families continue to observe certain native traditions that make the birth of a Lakota baby somewhat different from anywhere else. As with many Native American cultures, the umbilicus of the newborn infant is often kept as a sacred token and is placed in a special container and reserved for the child. The umbilicus represents the center of one's being and symbolizes the spiritual center of the sacred hoop of the world. Some Lakota say that a child must always keep this or know its whereabouts, or else his or her life will lack direction and meaning.

Because most women deliver their babies in the Rosebud Hospital, few continue to observe this tradition. However, the meaning is still recalled as the birth of the child is celebrated. Often a Giveaway is held to honor the birth of a baby, either by the parents or grandparents. On this occasion, gifts are given to those who gave presents to the baby. In this manner, gifts that have been made to the child are repaid, and the bonds of mutual aid are reinforced.

When a child reaches eight or ten years of age, a naming ceremony is often held at which the child is given an Indian name. Traditionally, children were re-named over and over throughout their lives, as their personalities developed. Names were chosen that seemed most descriptive of the children's characters or that symbolized desired qualities. Today, children receive western names at birth, but are often given an Indian name when their parents feel it is proper. This naming ceremony is a very serious event for the Lakota, and is usually presided over by a medicine man. Honoring songs, a Giveaway, and a feast all accompany the naming, at which time a feather is given to the child when the medicine man or elder bestows the chosen name. Traditional foods are almost always served, where other occasions may not require this—*wasna* (pemmican) is often passed around and eaten by all the observers. As with most other events, the host family prepares a feast for the invited public.

The naming of a child is looked upon seriously, as it was in the old days. People hope that the child will continue to behave in the manner that led to the selection of the name in the first place. Indian names often describe physical appearance as well as personality.

It is rare to meet a traditional, native-speaking Lakota who does not have an Indian name. Individuals are addressed by their Indian names in Lakota at rituals and social gatherings. The more assimilated Lakota tend to regard this practice as superfluous and they abandon it. There are many parents who themselves suffered teasing while away at boarding schools because of their Indian names. They are often reluctant to impose this on their children. Although it is always the adults' intention to instill pride in youngsters, Indian names can still be a common source of teasing by non-Indians at school. Names are intentionally corrupted or bastardized—a child named Night Shield might be called Day Shield, embarrassing or offending the child.

Often, when Indian names are spoken in English, they are altered by their being shortened to fit on official forms, receipts, and government documents. A name such as "Blue Horse" might be shortened to "Mr. Blue" or "Mr. Horse"; a couple with the name "Makes Room for Them" might become "Mr. and Mrs. Makes Room," and so on. The meanings of the names—and consequently their symbols—are forever lost.

Today, there are no rites of passage that mark puberty; however, young people are praised for their accomplishments and are publicly acknowledged with Giveaways for such things as high school graduation or completion of a job training program. Thus, the family not only honors its child but also thanks the community for their friendship and the help they have offered over the years. When an individual is successful at something, it is never considered his or her sole achievement; rather, is is seen that his or her effort *coupled with community support* has made it possible to achieve the desired goal.

Marriage, at one time acknowledged by reciprocal gift exchange between the couple's parents, is still publicly acknowledged by a Giveaway. Most young people get married in a church or civil ceremony, but very few have an elaborate formal ceremony or reception. Not only would the cost of such an event be extravagant, but few have homes where a reception could be held. But the basic reason big weddings are unpopular is that they are completely foreign. People talk frequently of getting married—marriage is a relationship of great importance in the indigenous culture—but it was always gift exchange rather than a wedding that marked the event.

Although ceremonies and social gatherings associated with death are structured within the framework of Christian churches, there are many Lakota elements that are part of the service and mourning. Most funeral arrangements are made through the tribe, which contracts with private mortuaries in Valentine, Nebraska, or Winner, South Dakota. But the funeral service is nearly always in the church that the family of the deceased attends. Arrangements generally include a wake of one to several nights, during which time friends come and sit with the family. The coffin and deceased are usually brought to the home, where friends and relatives can come during the wake and pay their last respects. Priests and ministers almost always officiate at funeral services, since this is not a traditional role of the medicine man. Later, at the Giveaway, both the clergymen and a medicine man will present eulogies. During the funeral service, hymns and prayers are often sung and spoken in the native language (see Chapter 6).

6 / Religion

6.1 RELIGIOUS COMPLEXITY AT ROSEBUD

Since the introduction of Christianity over a century ago, religious practices of the Lakota have been described as either Christian or native. While there may have been real differences between the two belief systems in the past, the space between them—both physical and conceptual—grows smaller and smaller. It is no longer accurate to interpret religious activity in this "either/or" manner. The compatibility and articulation of the two religious systems—Christianity and native religion—has been a source of great speculation and conjecture ever since the two systems came into contact. Some scholars claim that Lakota today participate simultaneously in two separate religious systems. Others claim that modern Lakota religion is a syncretic phenomenon, that is, that elements of native religion have merged with Christianity to produce a single unique religion. Still others suggest that modern Lakota participate in both native and Christian worship, but that each system contains numerous elements of the other.

For the Lakota at Rosebud, *all* of these characterizations are valid. For some, Christianity and native religion are indeed dissimilar, opposite ends of a continuum that will remain forever distant. It also seems to be the case that elements of Christianity *are* becoming more acceptable within the context of native practices, just as elements of native religion are being brought deliberately into the church. And yet, for the majority of Lakota, both systems are powerful forces that are becoming less distinct, more difficult to separate. There are many areas of religious life at Rosebud where a fusing of Christian and indigenous belief is, in fact, occurring.

As with all aspects of reservation life, Lakota do not represent a homogeneous group. Depending on the individual, the religious practitioner (shaman or priest), and the particular church, religious life is likely to fit into one of the following three categories:

1. The church and native ritual may be totally separate, having few, if any, points of articulation. Some individuals exclusively attend church and have nothing to do with indigenous practices. Likewise, some Lakota believe totally in the native ideology, attend only native rituals, and disavow any Christian elements that may inadvertently be introduced. For most people at Rosebud, exclusive religious participation is rare.

2. The church and native ritual are participated in equally but separately by some individuals. Whereas the church may be the most suitable religious institution for sponsoring baptisms, funerals, and wakes, native curing rituals may be considered the most effective means of diagnosing and recovering from illness. [This alternative is what Powers (1978) calls "dual organization" for the Pine Ridge Sioux; it is more realistically a dual *participation*.]

3. The Church and elements of native ritual may be merged in concept and in practice. Christian hymns in the native language, kneeling for Lakota supplicative prayer, and the fusion of the concept of God and *Wakan Tanka* are all examples of the way in which the two religious systems may be integrated.

The differences between Christianity and indigenous belief have been downplayed by the church to the extent that even symbolic meanings within one religious context now have meaning in the other. One Lakota expressed that the Sun Dance ritual was an enactment of Christ's sacrifice. There are numerous interpretations of both Christian and native concepts and symbols, and these continue to change as Lakota participate more fully in western life. The flow between religious systems is observed by MacGregor in his study of the Lakota at Pine Ridge:

> Belonging to a Christian church and attending Peyote or *Yuwipi* ceremonies bring no conflict to the Indian mind. Individuals pass from one group to another as the personalities of the leaders appeal to them or neighbors report unusual success in curing. The shift from one religion to another . . . becomes more understandable when it is realized that there are certain elements fundamental in the native pre-Christian religion which are carried over into the contemporary religions . . . seeking divine power for strength and assistance . . . for curing . . . a sense of security . . . and the sanctioning of a moral code (1946:102).

Before the complexities of religious worship can be discussed, it is necessary to outline the basic features of the traditional belief system. Only then can modern interpretations of these rituals be explained.

6.2   TRADITIONALISM

The native system of beliefs has undergone considerable modification in order to accommodate the stresses and strains of being Indian in a politically and economically complex world. Because the old religious traditions are such an essential part of being Lakota, reservation residents continue to cling to elements of the traditional culture and often rely on native explanations for modern events. In this way, even those who are not deeply religious still subscribe to a system of religious explanation that clearly stands apart from Judeo-Christian ideology. Traditional religion, then, is far more than style and form of ritual, but rather an outlook or a world view, a system of belief that shapes all activities and events. For some, native ideology penetrates every sphere of life. But for others, religion is becoming an increasingly segmented part of their lives. In contemporary reservation life, religion can play a strong role in maintaining social order, explaining unjust occurrences, accounting for all types of behavior, and helping to effect certain events.

Discussing religious life with Indian people today is not always an easy task. Investigators are generally regarded with suspicion and may be accused of "stealing" traditions by revealing them. When Lakota are willing to discuss their beliefs, the anthropologist is continually aware that at any time the conversation may suddenly cease, the investigator's questions perhaps touching on sensitive or private areas. Some Lakota will deny any knowledge of or participation in the traditional religion, out of a desire to discourage further inquiry. This device usually works, and the interviewer retreats. Other Lakota will discuss their beliefs; however, while they regard such topics of conversation as permissible, they nevertheless behave in a manner that shows they recognize a certain danger in discussing things *wakan* ("sacred, great"). The same attitude prevails concerning photography of any ritual events—it is too dangerous, and "the spirits" may become punitive. (See the discussion of the *yuwipi* cult in this chapter.)

Because of the tension surrounding religious topics, outsiders' questions concerning religion sometimes meet with odd looks, as though to say "How do *you* know about that?" Young people giggle and look around uncomfortably and elders may be evasive while discussing native ritual. People are careful to treat this subject with great sincerity and respect.

Although most Lakota have some degree of involvement with native religion, surprisingly few claim to be active participants, saying they rarely attend native rituals. Some communities are much more active in native ritual affairs than others. Spring Creek residents, for example, frequently attended ceremonies, whereas members of the Antelope community seldom did.

Cosmology and the Seven Sacred Rites

The native religion is based on a belief in a pantheon of gods or spirit powers who exercise control over all things in the universe. The Great Spirit, *Wakan Tanka*, heads all spirit powers in the pantheon and is currently considered to be both the equivalent to the monotheistic concept of God as well as the highest of sixteen powers who play important roles in the cosmology. Many Indian people were instructed by late nineteenth century missionaries that *Wakan Tanka* was equivalent to the Judeo-Christian concept of God, a convenient device for promoting the acceptance of Christianity, as noted by MacGregor:

> The Christian God was identified somewhat with the Dakota supernatural power through the missionaries' practice of calling God "*Wakan Tanka*" (1946: 92).

In the Lakota cosmology, the sacred powers are all subsumed under *Wakan Tanka* in four groups of four, as explained by Hassrick:

> The all-encompassing *Wakan Tanka* was conceived of in various graded levels of manifestation and was identified with each. . . . The number four was supremely important; and the idea of "many in one" is repeated again and again (1964:247).

At the head is *Wakan Tanka*, literally "sacred great/big," often referred to in English as the Great Mystery or Great Spirit. This great deity directly controls four major animistic forces or superior gods: *Inyan*, the Rock; *Maka*, the Earth; *Škan*, the Sky; and *Wi*, the Sun.

> Each of these had a special area of responsibility in the order of the universe. *Inyan* was the ancestor of all gods and all things; he was also the advocate of authority and the patron of the arts. *Maka*, who followed *Inyan* as the protector of the household, was believed to be the mother of all living things. *Škan*, who as the source of all force and power, sat in judgment on all the gods and spirits; and *Wi* . . . ranked first among them as the all-powerful Great God, defender of bravery, fortitude, generosity and fidelity (Hassrick 1964:247).

Each of these major forces has an associate, comprising the next level of gods, the associates: *Inyan* is associated with *Wakinyan*, the Winged, the patron of cleanliness and the symbol of thunder; *Maka* is associated with *Whope*, the Beautiful One, daughter of the Sun and Moon and patron of harmony and pleasure. *Škan* is associated with *Tate*, the Wind who controls the seasons. *Wi* is associated with *Hanwi*, the Moon, "who sets the time for important undertakings" (Hassrick 1964:247).

In addition, subordinate gods and godlike figures represent forces in the spirit world whose roles and controls are clearly spelled out in the origin myths and legends. The subordinates include the Buffalo, the Bear, the Four Winds, and the Whirlwind; godlike forces include the Spirit, Ghost, Spiritlike, and the Potency (Hassrick 1964:247).

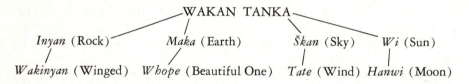

The superior gods and their associates

All sixteen deities are part of the Great Spirit, and are prayed to as part of the whole, since each controls different aspects of life. Prayer is very personalized among the Lakota, with the Earth often referred to as "Mother," the Sky as "Father," and *Wakan Tanka* as "Grandfather." In this manner, gods are not at all remote to individuals, but are extremely accessible forces, similar to kinsmen, and are addressed as such.

All forces in the cosmology are arranged in terms of the sacred numbers four and seven. Four represents the cardinal directions, while five, six, and seven represent zenith, nadir, and center. All of these are arranged in a sacred hoop or circle, which, to the Lakota, symbolizes the relationship among all living things. Within this continuous circle, all things are *wakan*, sacred, and therefore to be regarded with respect, reverence, and awe. Powers explains how belief is transformed into behavior for the Oglalas. It applies equally to the Brule at Rosebud:

> To the Oglalas, the totality of natural and cultural phenomena are capable of undergoing transformations which require that behavior toward these phe-

nomena be altered, or somewhat modified. The causes of these transformations and the Oglala explanation for concomitant changes in behavior are subsumed under the concept of *taku wakan,* "sacred things" (Powers 1977:45).

Traditional religion at Rosebud is based upon the use of the sacred pipe in a series of seven rituals, not all of which are still performed today. The Lakota believe that they did not always have the pipe or their current form of belief system; rather, their legends hold that a figure called the White Buffalo Calf Woman brought "the way of the pipe" to them, including prescriptions for its use and the seven sacred rites associated with it. The legendary transformation of this woman into a buffalo marked the beginning of a nomadic existence on the Plains and a dependence on the buffalo for the major necessities of life. Despite the fact that there is no longer any real economic dependence on the buffalo, the memory of this deep relationship between the Lakota and the buffalo is recalled continually even today. It is expressed in the use of the buffalo skull as a religious altar, the dragging of the buffalo skull in one form of the Sun Dance, the use of buffalo robes as beds for Sun Dance candidates to lie upon while being pierced, and on other religious occasions where there is some historical review of Lakota life.

Of the seven sacred rites brought to the Lakota, two may have been known to them prior to the coming of the White Buffalo Calf Woman: the Sweat Lodge ceremony or purification rite (*inikaǧapi,* literally "they purify themselves"), and Crying for a Vision or Vision Quest (*hanbleceyapi,* literally "they cry for a vision"). These two, along with the Sun Dance (*wiwanyang wacipi* or "sun gazing as they dance"), are performed regularly and continue to be an integral part of Lakota religious life. Before I discuss these major rituals in detail I will briefly describe the remaining four sacred rites.

Two ceremonies brought by the White Buffalo Calf Woman that have become nearly extinct are the Girls' Puberty Ritual (*isnati alowanpi,* "singing over first menses" (Hassrick 1964:297) and Throwing of the Ball (*tapa wankayeyapi,* "ball they throw high up") (Powers 1977, Brown 1971). The Girls' Puberty ceremony used to be performed on the fourth day of the Sun Dance, but is now rarely associated with Sun Dance affairs at Rosebud, although it is still performed occasionally at nearby Pine Ridge. Throwing of the Ball, or Buffalo Rite as it was also known (because the buffalo spirits guard a woman's chastity), was similar to the Girls' Puberty Ritual and was performed when the girl first began to menstruate. The ceremony was a recognition of the girl's emergence as a woman. She was taught women's skills such as quilling and making moccasins. At the end of a period of menstrual isolation, a Giveaway was held at which a ball was thrown and a large gift, such as a horse, was given to the person who caught the ball.

The Making of Relatives, *hunkayapi,* or "they call them *hunka*"—literally, *hunka* means "pipes," but it translates broadly as a wand or pipe that is waved over a person in making them a relative (Powers 1977:100)—and the Keeping of the Soul ceremony, *wanaǧi yuhapi* or *wakicaǧapi,* meaning "they keep the ghost," are less frequently held than major ceremonials like the Sun Dance, but do occasionally take place. The Making of Relatives ritual is held to establish a kinlike bond with a nonrelative, thus widening the circle of individuals upon whom one can depend. Powers states:

The purpose of the *Hunka* ritual is to create a bond between two people which is stronger than a kinship tie. The two people involved in this fictive relationship are obliged to die for each other if the need arises (1977:100).

Traditionally the ritual "involved the adoption of a younger and usually less wealthy individual by an older one, a relationship which required sharing through life on the part of both" (Hassrick 1964:297). Sometimes held to honor a child, the Making of Relatives ceremony establishes a highly formalized relationship. This ritual survives today because, even more than in precontact times, an individual is most likely to succeed with a maximum number of relatives, friends, and allies.

The Keeping of the Soul ceremony is observed only by the very traditional Lakota:

A ghost is kept so that by the proper rites it will be assured a return to its origin and because the lingering ghost will help people to be mindful of death (Powers 1977:93).

Immediately following a death, a lock of hair of the deceased is cut, wrapped, and kept for four days. During this period, the family is expected to be exceptionally quiet. The father is required to abide by certain restrictions, such as "not eating dog or any meat scraped from the hide of an animal" (Powers 1977:93). A ghost bundle is prepared, guarded, and "fed." The spirit (*wanaǧi*) of the deceased lingers "around its relatives until such time as it is ritually released" (Powers 1977:93). The ritual release takes place at the end of one year (some Lakota now observe this period of mourning for only six months). The ghost is fed for the last time. The family distributes its belongings at a feast or Giveaway, which releases them from their period of mourning, and they begin their life anew.

Whether or not a family "keeps the ghost" of their deceased relative, it is common practice to stage a Giveaway one year after a death. Although many modern Lakota believe that this period of waiting to give away is simply an appropriate period for commemorating the anniversary of a death, the year-long wait stems from the Keeping of the Soul ritual. Lakota who no longer formally observe this ceremony are still cautious about the four-day period immediately following a death. One informant stated:

You really have to be careful about what you do then. You can't do anything bad—like drink or steal—or that's what you'll be for the rest of your life.

The three remaining ceremonies—Sweat Lodge, Vision Quest, and Sun Dance—currently constitute the core of contemporary Lakota ceremonialism. Although these are traditional ceremonies, elements of them have been changed through acculturation.

The Sweat Lodge Ceremony is considered one of, if not *the,* oldest ritual in Lakota culture. Sometimes it is performed as a rite unto itself; it also may be held as a preparatory cleansing step for another ritual, such as the *yuwipi* or the *lowanpi* curing rituals, the Sun Dance, or the Vision Quest. The purpose of the Sweat Lodge ritual is not just physical cleansing, but spiritual purification. Both men and women may participate in this ritual. The Sweat Lodge ritual is held in a willow-sapling frame structure covered with canvas tarps. The entrance typically faces east, although it may be in any of the four directions, depending on the vision of the medicine man. To the east of the Sweat Lodge is the sacred path to the fire containing heated rocks, which are brought into the lodge (Brown 1971: 32–33). The water that is poured over the rocks, the rocks themselves, and the willow saplings are all symbolic of *wakan* ("sacred, powerful") forces and create a solemn environment for prayer, the entreatment of spirits that enter, and the smoking of the sacred pipe. Even today, the Sweat Lodge ceremony is a means of diagnosing the sincerity of individuals wishing to undergo the Sun Dance ritual. The medicine man can detect if the candidate is free of evil or confused thoughts during this most sacred event. If a candidate's motives are questionable or if he or she is skeptical or uncertain, the medicine man prevents further par-

Prayers offered on a solitary hill may bring a vision of spiritual guidance to the supplicant. (photograph courtesy of the Nebraska Curriculum Institute for Native American Life)

ticipation of the individual until clarity of heart and mind have been achieved. (For more detailed description of the Sweat Lodge ceremony, see Brown 1971, Powers 1977.)

Like the Sweat Lodge ceremony, the Vision Quest, *hanblečeyapi,* is conducted both as a ceremony unto itself and also as a preparatory step in the performance of the annual Sun Dance. An individual wishing to seek a vision approaches a medicine man with whom he begins a long relationship of religious and moral tutelage. To cement the bond between them, the individual obtains a pipe, which he makes himself, has made, or purchases. He presents it to his mentor and discusses with him his intention to seek a vision. The medicine man may accept or decline the offer. If he accepts, a long period of guidance and instruction begins. Traditionally this was a year; today, however, the time period varies depending on the needs of the individual. During the actual Vision Quest, a young man (women may, but rarely do, seek a vision) climbs a hill that has been specified as a sacred place and, with his pipe, prays to the supernatural forces:

> A person undertakes a Vision Quest to gain power or to seek a vision which will help explain unsolicited visions or to help prophesy the outcome of a hunting or war expedition (Powers 1977:91).

Permitted no food and water, the supplicant is in the proper frame of mind to have a dream or vision. Traditionally, the Vision Quest continued for four days and nights, but today the amount of time spent depends on the person's—or the spirits'—choice. It may last for the full four-day period, but if the spirits designate that it should last only a morning or evening, this is what is done. Not all seekers receive a vision; in fact, few do. The vision is a special source of power often accompanied by specific ritual instructions, songs, and personal guidance in the form of animals, figures, or thunder. Often this power can be called upon for assistance, and songs obtained in this manner can be sung for protection or assistance, as when the candidate is attempting to break free of his bonds during the Sun Dance. Sometimes during the Vision Quest an individual receives a calling to become a medicine man. He is obligated to follow this ritual prescription. Carter (1966) indicates that a person who refuses to acknowledge this calling may be burdened later in life and may become *heyoka,* a clown, who lives in "an antinatural manner" (Powers 1977:93). Carter explains:

> A dream of the Thunderbirds can also be fulfilled by joining the Heyoka cult, and this is one of the "escapes" for people who do not wish to become involved in shamanistic activities (1966:62).

Whether or not a vision is achieved and regardless of what type of vision is obtained, the goal of the Vision Quest for a Sun Dance candidate is "to convince the supernatural sources of power that the candidate humbly desires their assistance and is worthy of its reception" (Carter 1966:63). The quality of self-sacrifice is not restricted to the Vision Quest, but plays a large role as well, in the Sun Dance.

For many modern Lakota men, seeking a vision is a process by which they validate their identity. For in the process, they learn the Lakota lore and moral teachings. More importantly, individuals who undergo this experience often regain clarity of purpose in their lives and a secure identity as a member of their tribe. Today, both men and women participate in the Vision Quest for all kinds of reasons: for thanksgiving, to ask for spiritual guidance, or simply for solitary prayer.

The Sun Dance

Of all the ceremonial rituals of the Lakota, the Sun Dance is the most spectacular. "No one other ceremonial of Teton Dakota culture is as characteristic of that culture as is the Sun Dance" (Feraca 1963:11). It used to be performed annually at the time of the summer buffalo hunt when members of the Teton bands reunited. Currently it is held between mid-July and early August. The Sun Dance is not only a declaration of individual bravery and fortitude—traditionally valued highly by the Lakota—but is also the supreme rite of intensification for the society as a whole. Candidates who undergo the Sun Dance do so to fulfill a vow that they have made. For example, one might vow to undergo this rite of self-torture if a sick relative recovered or if a relative or friend currently in military service returned safely. In contemporary times, the Sun Dance is regarded as a way of uniting the Lakota people in a ritual of self-awareness, political consciousness, and common identity. During the 1972 Sun Dance at Pine Ridge, a member of the American Indian Movement proudly asserted that this ritual was a prayer for the communal well-being and prosperity of the Lakota people.

Only men participate in the piercing; women can participate in the Sun Dance either as supporters of a particular candidate, or to fulfill a vow that they themselves have made. The customary manner for women to participate is by giving flesh offerings—bits of flesh generally cut from the arms. For both men and women the ceremony currently is an intense four-day ritual preceded by physical and spiritual preparation. Formerly, such preparation took twelve days. The modern abbreviation takes into account that Saturday and Sunday are the most practical days for the public to attend morning rituals.

The initial step in preparing for the Sun Dance is the selection of a tall, straight cottonwood tree to be used as the Sun Dance pole. It is selected ceremonially; the final blow to fell the tree is struck by a woman, a virgin, symbolic of the White Buffalo Calf Woman. Specific songs and prayers accompany the cutting and transporting of the tree. When the tree is brought to the Sun Dance lodge, a hole is dug in the ground. In it may be placed tobacco offerings, some buffalo fat, and perhaps a sacred pipe. The tree is then hoisted and tied with ropes and cloth banners. A cluster of sixteen cherry sticks, symbolic of the nest of the powerful Thunderbird, is put in the top of the tree; in it are placed tobacco offerings. Effigies of a buffalo, symbolizing that which has given all life to the Lakota, and a man on a horse (made of either rawhide or cardboard) are also placed in the tree, some-times including an arrow for buffalo-killing and a picket pin for securing a captured horse (Hassrick 1964). A reddened buffalo or calf skin and cotton banners of the four sacred colors are then tied to branches of the tree. By tradition, each color symbolizes one of the four cardinal directions. Some contemporary medicine men say that the colors symbolize the four races of mankind, but this explanation is a modern one.

Before the twentieth century, the Sun Dance was considered a drama enacting
the symbolic capture, torture, and release of the enemy. Young men went through
the Sun Dance annually to demonstrate their bravery as though they themselves
had been captured and tortured, finally struggling to obtain their freedom. The
practice of piercing the flesh of the individual by thongs attached to ropes tied to
the Sun Dance pole and the subsequent breaking free certainly does bring to mind
the traditional imagery. People on the reservation no longer give this explanation
for the Sun Dance; in fact, many do not even know of it.

Several forms of the Sun Dance existed in the past, most of which are still performed today. In the first, "gazing at the sun" (Walker 1917, Powers 1977), the
candidate gazes at the sun from dawn to dusk, but is not pierced. This is the form
currently chosen by young initiates who are participating for the first time. The
second form and the one most frequently selected today, "pierced," requires that
the skin over the pectoral muscles be pierced, on one or both sides, and a skewer
inserted. A thong is then wrapped around the skewer and attached to a rope, the
other end of which has been secured about halfway up the pole. After struggling
to free himself, the dancer breaks free of his bonds. The third form, "suspended,"
involves piercing both the chest and upper back (shoulder) area. The dancer,
suspended between four poles, writhes about until he is able to free himself of all
four ropes. I observed one instance of a variation of this form. The dancer was
pierced above both breasts and, once attached to ropes, stepped up on a man who
was kneeling on his hands and knees. The kneeling man withdrew, leaving the
candidate to hang suspended until his skewers tore free. Many Lakota regard this
"suspended" form as the ultimate in reverence for the traditional ways. Others
regard it as sensationalistic and eccentric and they question the sincerity of those
who choose this most painful form. The fourth form, "dragging buffalo skulls,"
involves piercing the flesh on the back shoulder area. A skewer is inserted from

*Preparation for the Sun Dance begins with an early morning Sweat Lodge
ceremony.*

which a thong, rope, and buffalo skull are tied (Dorsey 1894:461). The candidate drags the skull around the Sun Dance shade area until it tears loose. This form is less popular than the front "pierced" form. Another way in which the candidate "pierced" involved a horse pulling away from the dancer until he broke free.

The contemporary four-day ceremony usually begins on Thursday with the Sweat Lodge ritual. On Friday and Saturday the spectators observe the symbolic presentation, acceptance, and return of the sacred pipe between candidate and mentor. The piercing usually takes place on Sunday.

A medicine man raises his razor blade to the sky for blessing prior to the piercing.

Women sound a trill of victory and support as a Sun Dancer tries to break free of his bonds.

With rare exceptions, the pipe is always publicly accepted in the Sweat Lodge ritual, declaring the individual worthy of undergoing the Sun Dance. I have witnessed several occasions in which the pipe was refused. The candidate was then instructed to approach the medicine man again, this time kneeling and crawling in extreme humility. There is no evidence that this was done in the past; rather, it seems to represent one particular medicine man's contemporary interpretation of the Christian posture of kneeling as a gesture of humility. Each individual offers his pipe to his mentor four times. The first three offers are rejected and the fourth is generally accepted. Once the pipe ceremony is complete, final approval is granted for the candidate to undergo the self-torture.

Accompanied by singing and drumming, each individual is pierced in the fashion he has chosen, either with razor or knife, and dances at his place until all candidates have been pierced and attached to the Sun Dance pole. Finally, the medicine man shouts *"Hokahe!"*—"Let's go!"—and all the men approach the tree. They do this three times, all the while praying to the sacred tree for a quick release. The fourth time the signal to advance is given, the men approach the tree and then quickly run away from it, tearing free of their bonds and often falling from

A medicine man and Sun Dancer, having broken free of his bonds, receives his pipe back from the singers and drummers.

the tremendous momentum built up in running. Those who do not break free must try again, for it is considered dishonorable to have one's skewer and rope removed. Frequently children or relatives will join in the effort to break free by clasping the hands of the candidate and running with them, adding weight and usually succeeding in breaking free. While no one may ask for the skewer to be *removed,* it is honorable to ask to be *cut* free. In an account of the 1866 Sun Dance, George Hill describes a candidate who, unable to break free, "called two friends and gave each a pony in the presence of the lookers-on to cut them off which they did" (Paige 1979:107).

Following the release, Sun Dancers and medicine men congratulate each other while women in the Sun Dance lodge trill a sound of victory. Finally the pipes are returned to each of the candidates and the ordeal officially ends. Those wishing to make a vow to go through the Sun Dance in subsequent years are asked to step forward and publicly declare their intentions.

Spectators have an opportunity to congratulate the dancers and also the privilege to have these brave men say a prayer for them. In a brief contemporary ritual called the "Blessing Ceremony," two lines form, one of Sun Dancers and one of spectators. Each dancer touches the top of the head of a spectator, sometimes fanning them with a ceremonial eagle feather fan, and says a prayer for the spectator.

Today's Attitudes toward the Sun Dance

Although the Sun Dance is the most sacred and elaborate of Lakota rituals, there is often disagreement among reservation residents as to whose form of performance is correct, whose is too commercialized, or whose is most sacred. Because of this local disagreement, some Sun Dances are poorly attended. Different factions sponsor their own Sun Dance, so there may be as many as three or four in a given summer. This is not surprising since there is considerable variability in the style of each medicine man. Powers' observations of the Sun Dance at Pine Ridge apply equally to the ritual at Rosebud:

> I have personally attended fourteen sun dances at Pine Ridge. Between the literature and my own observations it becomes obvious that no two sun dances have ever been performed quite the same since 1950 and perhaps they never were (1977:139).

Today, complaints of a lack of standardization have been brought to the attention of a council of medicine men and their associates at Rosebud. This group of individuals now hold their own Sun Dance as a way of continuing the style and version of the ritual that they feel is most traditional.

The question of whether there should be many or just one official Sun Dance is not the only bone of contention in the celebration of modern rituals. Disagreements occur concerning almost every aspect and cause dissension and ill-will in the community. Such criticisms account for poor attendance. Some of the issues include arguments about payment of a fee to a medicine man performing the piercing. While some wish to be paid through the Sun Dance committee, others believe the acceptance of such a fee is evidence of commercialization. The location of the Sun Dance is also an area for disagreement. The Rosebud Tribal Fairgrounds has been a popular spot for the ritual, but many Lakota are unwilling to support a Sun Dance held there if it is also used for powwow dancing in the evenings. Since the Sun Dance is a strictly sacred ritual, use of the fairgrounds is considered by some to be irreverent and disrespectful. Hence, they do not attend.

One frequently hears complaints by spectators concerning photographing and taping of the Sun Dance. The Lakota are divided on this topic, too. Some believe that no taping or photographing whatsoever should be permitted. Others believe that recording of the proceedings is acceptable if the slides, photographs, tapes, or films are used for educational purposes, such as at the Sinte Gleska College on the reservation. Still others believe that recording should be permitted only if substantial donations are made; however, this is considered by some to be bribery. No matter what decision is made about taping or filming a particular Sun Dance, there are always critics.

More and more, elderly Lakota are concerned about changes in the ritual, the fact that "it's just not being performed right, the way it used to be."

Despite the varying degrees of hostility to the Sun Dance displayed by the Teton who camp by the thousands on the grounds, there are many spectators. The Teton are interested if only to observe "how badly they're doing it" (Feraca 1963:18).

For instance, Sun Dance candidates are supposed to fast, but do not always do so. Spectators criticize the leaders of the ritual for not enforcing strict adherence to these traditions. As early as 1963, Feraca noted:

In recent years many accusations have been heaped on the heads of those participants in the dance, including singers who have been seen eating and drinking during the ceremony. At one ceremony I observed the singers eating watermelon during the rest periods, at the same time complaining about a white visitor with a loud and raucous voice (1963:18).

Speeches that used to be made in Lakota at Sun Dance rituals are now often made in English, or at the very least, an English translation is offered. While fewer Lakota object to this (many young people do not speak or understand the native language), there is still criticism of assimilative influences.

The effects of changes in the Sun Dance are strongly felt in the community. In addition to political factions, the community is divided attitudinally into "purists" and "progressives," native speakers versus non-native, militants versus non-militants —they are split along every possible line. Powers discusses similar problems for the Pine Ridge Sioux:

The crass commercialism of the sacred rite has been the subject of criticism by traditional purists, and the tribal council has been accused of sensationalizing the "torture" of the sun dance in an attempt to draw more tourists. The commercialism has also tended to underscore the extant factionalism between the full-bloods and mixed-bloods, at least politically and economically (Powers 1977:140).

The discontent, lack of support, and sometimes outright disinterest in public events drives deeper wedges between the young, who desire knowledge and experience in traditional life, and the elderly, who are the cultural links to the past.

Despite the divisiveness, continued observance of this ritual has significant positive effects, especially on the young. Many young people have begun to take an interest in indigenous tradition and have experienced a religious and cultural reawakening. Young men who are unfamiliar with the traditional culture are undertaking a period of tutelage with a medicine man in order to become better acquainted with native tradition. This is especially important for the adolescents and young adults who cannot sense their place in the traditional Lakota world. Many men and women suffering from alcoholism find renewed strength and pride in their new spiritual life and begin to straighten out their lives. Without question, participation in the Sun Dance today gives young people a new alternative—to get involved in being Lakota, to determine for themselves what being an Indian means, and to begin to experience a sense of self-worth they may never have known before.

The Yuwipi Cult

All the religious ceremonies at Rosebud revolve around an attempt to contact supernatural powers to utilize or harness their help. The *yuwipi* cult is considered by some to be the only continuing cult of the Dakota religion involved in this manipulation (MacGregor 1946:98). Currently, the rituals that are performed the most frequently and with the greatest regularity both at Rosebud and Pine Ridge are the *yuwipi* and *lowanpi* ceremonies, which are organized primarily for the purpose of curing. Although many historians and anthropologists consider *yuwipi* to be a separate cult, it is really a specific form of the more generalized *lowanpi* healing ritual.

> Broadly speaking, *Yuwipi* is a generic term which includes a number of variants of curing rituals, all of which are held in a darkened room and are conducted by specialists known locally as *yuwipi wičasa,* "Yuwipi man" (Powers 1977:144).

These rituals have been described in detail by Kemnitzer (1970), Feraca (1963), and Powers (1977). They define *yuwipi* literally as "they wrap him up" or "they roll it up," referring to the practice of "binding the shaman and his release by the spirits during the performance in a dark room" (Kemnitzer 1970:40). Membership in this cult is determined by attendance and participation at meetings, held frequently throughout the year. Blankets and quilts are placed over windows and doors to exclude all light, for the spirits appear in the dark as white flashes of light. *Lowanpi,* literally "they sing," is the broader type of ritual in which supernatural spirits are entreated for diagnosing, healing, or curing. However, no wrapping or binding of the shaman occurs, and this ceremony is usually not performed in the dark.

The most common reasons for holding either of these two ceremonies are recovery of a lost object, diagnosis of illness, supplication of supernatural spirits, curing the sick, praying for someone's welfare—whether the person is in the military service or has emigrated to an urban area and is down on luck—and to find an answer to a mysterious question, for example, who is responsible for an unsolved crime. One very common reason to request a ceremony is to pray for someone who is severely alcoholic and whose life is endangered by the ill effects of this disease. These two rituals are held so frequently that it is unusual not to hear of one occurring every week. Despite predictions that this cult would disappear among the young (MacGregor 1946), ceremonies continue to be arranged by young and old alike.

Both *yuwipi* and *lowanpi* ceremonies may be performed by two types of shaman or ritual specialists—the *wapiye wičasa* or "medicine man," or the *ieska,* literally "interpreter." Often herbs and medicinal remedies are used in effecting cures. Reservation residents commission the medicine men whom they believe perform the most effective ceremonies. Some will say of a particular medicine man, "Oh, he's not really traditional; he's not a real medicine man." Although there are differences in styles among medicine men, strict adherence to a particular ritual form is necessary. It is largely a matter of personal preference and success of outcome as to which medicine men are most highly regarded. Medicine men are generally not paid in money for performing these rituals. Instead, in the Lakota spirit of reciprocity, most ceremonial sponsors will present a gift to the medicine man as well as provide all the food necessary to feed those in attendance. Traditionally, boiled dog was served at these events, but today pork, beef, or chicken is prepared. The food served may also depend on the vision of the medicine man holding the ceremony. Dogs had to be ritually prepared by strangulation, by singeing of the hair, and by ritual quartering prior to being boiled. Dog is considered a rare culinary delicacy nowadays, especially by elderly Lakota. Young people eat dog ceremonially, but usually joke considerably about it (not at the ceremony). They are uncomfortable with non-Indian criticism of the practice.

Great care is taken to prevent any type of contamination during a ritual. Non-Indians may attend, but if they are not true believers, at least they must not be disbelievers. They must remain open, receptive, and willing to learn. Any skepticism will be sufficient cause for the ceremony to fail. Precautions are taken to exclude menstruating women for fear of contamination. While Lakota women are aware of this taboo, non-Indian women seldom are. Consequently, they are often blamed for an unsuccessful meeting. Menstruating women are denied attendance because they are especially powerful and may alter the course of the ceremony, possibly damaging herbs or medicines. One Lakota explained that menstrual flow symbolizes what might have been a living child; its passage from the woman is therefore symbolic of the death of the fetus and its expulsion from the woman. This association with death is considered far too dangerous in contacting supernatural spirits.

The persistence of the *yuwipi* cult is not surprising, considering how highly adaptable the ceremonies are to contemporary life. Whether curing illness or dispelling misfortune caused by spirits or alcohol, *yuwipi* meetings remain effective means of helping people control their lives. MacGregor wrote in 1946, "This cult will probably continue for a long time. . . ." (p. 103). But he also predicted that ceremonies would decrease as influence "with the world outside the reservation" increased (p. 103). In fact, thirty years later, the cult appears to be as strong as ever. Feraca notes for Pine Ridge:

> A South Dakota State College Bulletin describes *Yuwipi* as marginal to Sioux religions and in that sense to be equated with the Peyote Cult (Malan and Jesser 1959:48–49). In this I must disagree. *Yuwipi* is very widespread and embodies all the basic elements of Teton Dakota cultism (1963:26).

The reasons for its continuing popularity at Rosebud are explored in the following section.

Contemporary Interpretations of Indigenous Religion

Some modern interpretations of traditional religious practices have appeared in the preceding section. However, the application of native religion to all, even non-religious, aspects of daily life shows how the native ideology has been adapted to modern life rather than discarded as obsolete.

The belief in supernatural spirits is an integral part of Lakota belief. Spirits are believed to be everywhere and can appear at any time, whether ritually summoned or not. To most individuals, these spirits appear as flashing white or blue lights, often accompanied by high shrieking sounds that are deafening and extremely frightening. These spirits have boundless power—indeed, they can even untie a medicine man who has been wrapped in a quilt secured with leather thongs. These spirits play an important role in social control. Many individuals believe in a system of immanent justice or supernatural retribution effected by spirits. It is people's belief in supernatural controlling agents that may dissuade them from committing an act of wrongdoing. Some Indian people feel that, despite the ineffectiveness of law enforcement, social order is maintained because individuals fear supernatural retribution from spirits if their conduct is at all improper. So spirits are perceived as a mechanism that, ultimately, protects them against potential harm.

Another more active use of traditional belief is in *wakunza,* the attempt to use supernatural spirits to effect a particular outcome of some event. This may take the form of casting a hex or curse on an individual either as a threat to, or as punishment for, malicious or dangerous behavior, or it may take a positive form, that is, summoning spirits to help an individual. In the event of a wrongdoing, the victim utters a hex in Lakota to the effect that any person causing evil or unjust events will be punished drastically, perhaps by death. Even if a hex is not cast, infraction of the moral order will still be punished by spiritual forces. It is people's knowledge of this system of divine retribution that acts as a deterrent against more crimes being committed than are already. Many Indian people regard certain dangerous events as warnings, and, recognizing them quickly, correct their behavior before a serious tragedy befalls them. Several examples illustrate this belief in supernatural interventions as warnings by spirits.

Carter cites in his study of shamanism on the Lower Brule Reservation (1966) an incident in which a shaman's car broke down, but the medicine man was only slightly upset. When asked about his apparent indifference, he replied:

> Oh, I knew something like this would happen. That sweatbath we had last week was no good, the one when I let HF go in after he had been drinking. I know I wasn't supposed to do that. Something like this always happens after those things (Carter 1966:91).

Another incident at Rosebud involved a young woman who sought a cure for her disquiet about spirits:

> During the summer of 1973, a woman on the Rosebud Reservation spoke of feeling afraid at night and not being able to sleep because of hearing mysterious sounds. Deciding to consult her grandmother, she was told that she suffered at

night because she was being punished by the spirits—that she had done something wrong and was being warned. Uncomfortable with the fear of potential punishment, she consulted a holy man who held a *yuwipi* meeting for her. At the close of the ceremony, she was given a sacred stone and was told to use it in prayer to relieve her anxiety. After the meeting, her fears were allayed (Grobsmith 1974:131).

Spirits are credited with knowing when rituals are performed improperly and can be vindictive and punitive against transgressors. For example, if a menstruating woman attends a *yuwipi* meeting, the spirits may punish her by making her sick. Or the person for whom the meeting is being held may become ill. At the very least, the medicines or herbs to be used by the healer will become brown, ruined, and totally ineffective. Spirits, then, are not only blamed when things go awry; they are also credited with keeping things morally in order and seeing that human beings, in their mortal errors, do not make too big a mess of things.

The native system of logic—if you make mistakes, you pay for them—applies equally to non-Indians living in the Indian community. My own loss of several objects within a single week was explained as a warning by the spirits of some improper event in my life. Most of my friends suggested a supernatural explanation for my personal misfortune.

The native religion is often the only real source of comfort and cure from the ills that plague modern reservation life. Accident, homicide, and suicide rates are all high. An undertaker who lives near the reservation estimated that half of the deaths on the reservation occurred from such nonnatural causes. People tend to turn to native religion when things are going badly for them. They believe that traditional cures are the only truly effective means of ridding themselves of social ills.

When a family goes to a medicine man to help turn the tide of events, it is usually to summon all the supernatural support possible to bring about a change in the afflicted person. Most often, the affliction is alcoholism. Alcohol-related traffic accidents are a frequent occurrence and leave a residue of problems such as orphaned children, permanent disability, temporary unemployment due to injury, and, at the very least, loss of the family's only means of transportation. If a family suffers numerous misfortunes within a short time, they assume these incidents are warnings of worse things to come if the situation is not corrected. They seek the help of a medicine man to discover the source of the problem, hoping to avoid further misfortune. There is a strong sense of causal relationship: things do not just happen, they are brought on by certain behavior. Supernatural assistance can identify the behavior, cause it to cease, and return things to their proper order.

Theft is a reason for seeking the assistance of a medicine man. One of the traditional functions of the *lowanpi* meeting is to locate lost objects. Consultation with a medicine man and holding a ceremony may reveal the identity of the thief, the location of the lost goods, and perhaps the means to retrieve them. Even if no financial satisfaction or reimbursement is attained, knowledge of who committed the crime renders the victim informed, enlightened, and the wiser. One Lakota recounted an incident involving the theft of a sum of cash that had been placed in a small beaded coin purse. The medicine man whose assistance she sought instructed her to go home and look in her immediate surroundings for evidence of the theft. She found the stolen empty coin purse in a neighbor's trash. Although she was unable to recover the money, she was grateful to know the identity of the thief so that she could protect herself in the future.

6.3   THE NATIVE AMERICAN CHURCH

Since the late nineteenth century the use of peyote in rituals of the Peyote Cult, or what is now called the Native American Church of North America, has become more widespread. The spread of this religion to the Plains region has produced very different results in different Indian communities. Peyote reached the Omaha and Winnebago on the Nebraska reservations in 1906 and was rapidly integrated. The Peyote church now has a large following there. It then spread to the Sioux at Rosebud and other northern Plains reservations, where it has not gained acceptance. It was not even officially organized at Rosebud until 1924. Feraca points out that, of all the Plains tribes, the Teton were one of the last groups to embrace the cult. In fact, they (Brule) "cannot be considered peyote users as the Comanche and other Oklahoma groups" can (Feraca 1963:48).

Peyote reached the Plains area via the Southern tribes of Oklahoma, to whom it had spread from Mexico. Hertzberg states:

> The ancestry of the new movement reached far back into pre-Columbian times . . . among the Indians of Mexico. Its first appearance in the United States seems to have been around 1870 when it was acquired from Indians in Northern Mexico by the Mescalero Apaches. . . . The Comanche acquired it in 1873 or 1874 and the Iowa about 1875. Both tribes were important in its subsequent diffusion among Indians in the United States (1971:240–241).

Early Indian followers of the religion, such as Quanah Parker and John Wilson, preached its value: the rejection of infidelity, gambling, and alcohol; and direct communication with God (rather than through Jesus Christ). Its character was distinctly Christian—specifically Protestant—representing a mixture of Indian and Christian philosophical beliefs.

Ceremonies continue to be conducted by a leader or "road chief," who is assisted by a "drummer" and "fire chief." Participants pray in English and the native language of the local Indian community. Each participant sings four peyote songs, accompanying him- or herself with a gourd rattle, while someone else plays the drum. When the participant finishes, he or she passes on the rattle, and someone else begins to sing, requesting another to accompany them on the drum. The drum and rattle are passed around until everyone has sung.

Peyote, a bitter-tasting cactus button that contains the hallucinogen mescaline, is passed around and eaten in the form of a paste and a tea. Although it makes people feel very nauseated, they rarely excuse themselves from the meeting. To alleviate the discomfort, each person holds a tin can into which he retches.

The ceremony usually lasts all night and is followed by a feast in the morning. Participants make testimonials and pray aloud in the native language and English, seeking guidance in solving their problems. The hallucinogenic properties of peyote enable participants to have revelations that are cures or answers to their prayers. Native American Church meetings are held for the same reasons most *yuwipi* meetings are arranged: to cure illness (peyote is considered a panacea), to improve one's personal circumstances, or to give thanks.

It is only recently that ceremonies of the Native American Church have been legally permitted. In 1917 and 1918, various states passed antipeyote laws, and the transportation or use of peyote was considered a crime. Many anthropologists were called by the government as expert witnesses in claims cases to testify on behalf of Native American use of peyote. After years of antipeyote campaigning by state and federal governments, the ban on peyote was lifted and its use permitted only in chartered churches of the Native American Church of North America.

It is not difficult to see why peyotism gained wide acceptance among some Native American tribes. Its ethical code offered a way of life that promised more peaceful times to tribal groups who had been dislocated and were undergoing severe acculturative stress. Peyotism became extremely popular among the Navajo, particularly in the period following the devastating effects of stock (primarily sheep) reduction from 1934 to 1950. Using peyote as a sacrament, Indians urgently desired the results this new religion preached: brotherly love, care of the family, self-reliance, and temperance (Aberle 1966:13–14). Its popularity lay in its rejection of full assimilation into the white man's world, and its retention of a distinctly Indian manner of worship. The Omaha and Winnebago tribes in the Plains, relocated several times and reduced in number, relied on peyotism as a way of clinging to their native culture. For the Lakota, however, the cult did *not* represent the primary avenue for preserving their indigenous practices. Despite the Religious Crimes Code of 1906 and the government's forbidding the practice of certain rituals (the Sun Dance was prohibited in 1881 and was officially banned until 1933), native ceremonies continued to be held, albeit underground. The huge population of Sioux in the Dakota territory reduced the impact of religious assimilation. Among all the different bands of Sioux, some level of native activity was constant.

Peyotism is practiced by a few Lakota at Rosebud, but the popularity of the Native American Church is surprisingly low. Those who do participate tend to be mostly from the very traditional communities. Young people, frequently considered militant by conservative Lakota, are becoming more interested in the Native American Church, but the attraction of some members of the American Indian Movement to this church has, in turn, frightened away many conservative adults. Other individuals say they simply do not need this church—that they have their own religion. They recognize that peyotism is a recently acquired religion for their people, and that it does not truly reflect their native beliefs.

Indifference to peyotism has been observed elsewhere for the Sioux. MacGregor noted Oglala skepticism about the cult at Pine Ridge:

> Indian non-members of the cult . . . generally regard it as a menace that causes laziness and depletes families' wealth (1946:100).

MacGregor also noted the lack of peyotists in the town of Pine Ridge and attributed this partly to the strong influence of the Christian churches. The same is true for Rosebud, for the trancelike states induced by peyote are considered eccentric and potentially hazardous. The lack of popularity of peyotism in Rosebud is reinforced by Lakota resentment of the influx of vision-seeking hippies in the 1960s. Although hippies were not responsible for the use of peyote at Rosebud, it was rapidly associated with them. By the 1970s, this situation seemed to have been resolved.

6.4 CHRISTIANITY AT ROSEBUD

For most anthropologists, non-Indians, educators, and others, Christianity is strictly nonnative and purely acculturative, and has been grafted onto the indigenous belief system. Looking at contemporary Rosebud, it is difficult to imagine the community without the Christian church. Christian thought and practices have thoroughly penetrated native life—to the point that it appears to *be* indigenous. Today, over one hundred years have passed since the missionaries began their work among the Lakota, and there have been three generations in which the Indian people have become increasingly dedicated to their churches.

A brief look at the history of the Christian church at Rosebud will reveal the very deep if ambivalent relationship between the Indians and the church and the secure place the church occupies in most people's lives. This relationship is a paradoxical one, for the church was both an aggressor in attempting to "civilize" the Indians, and, at the same time, the only group continuously offering aid and hope during a period of rapid economic change. Although missionaries may have capitalized on a situation ideal for introducing a new religion, the Indian people recognized that those missionaries were not themselves to blame for the changes; on the contrary, their sympathetic assistance was deeply appreciated and still is to this day.

Following the treaty-making period (1850–71), the U.S. government's Indian policy promoted assimilation into mainstream American life. Schools, farm equipment, agricultural assistance, and livestock were provided. President Ulysses S. Grant encouraged churches to become involved in this task of "civilizing" the Indian. During his administration, reservations were assigned to particular religious denominations, a policy that became known as Grant's Peace Policy. Ten years later, President Hayes reinstituted governmental control over reservations and reversed Grant's policy, returning the responsibility for control over the Indians to government agents. But in the 1880s, reservations were once again opened up to religious sects wishing to set up schools and missions. This time, however, any church wishing to set up a mission on a reservation was permitted to do so. This exposed the Indians to a wider range of denominations, which often competed for membership. At the same time, the Dawes Allotment Act of 1887 divided Indian lands into 160-acre parcels per family (80 acres per individual). The breakup of tribal land holdings and massive pressures to assimilate, combined with the churches' efforts to convert and "civilize" the Indians, created a quarter century of change that had more drastic consequences on Indian culture than any other period in the history of Indian–white contact.

After reservations had officially been created at Pine Ridge and Rosebud in 1878, Presbyterian, Episcopal, and Roman Catholic missions were established there. The earliest mission at Rosebud was St. Mary's Episcopal Mission, established in 1874 by Bishop William H. Hare, who was "at the agency as head of a special commission appointed by the President to settle the Sioux problem" (Olson 1965:167). Later it was renamed the Bishop Hare School and became known as "the Mission," the present site of the town of Mission, South Dakota, now the largest town on the reservation. The St. Francis Mission, a Catholic mission and boarding school, was established eleven years later (1885), seven miles southwest of the agency town of Rosebud. Both missions created educational facilities for Indian children. Later, missionaries from the Mormon Church and the Church of God also arrived upon the scene.

The high degree to which Christianity has been assimilated into native life is surprising, considering its low acceptance initially:

> The missionaries created resistance by trying to eradicate the native religion instead of using it as a frame of reference in which to introduce Christianity. They attempted to impose Christian morality by suppressing Indian custom. . . . They tried to drive out indiscriminately Indian ways which had no relation to religion in the Indian mind (MacGregor 1946:92).

Succeeding generations have made their peace with Christianity and most people at Rosebud now belong to a Christian sect. In 1963, 60 percent of the Lakota at Pine Ridge and Rosebud were members of the Catholic Church, "the rest . . . divided among Protestant groups, and a few officially listed as members of the Native American or Peyote church" (Feraca 1963:7). MacGregor notes the same phenomenon:

> Since the coming of the first missionaries among the Teton-Dakota . . . the resistance or indifference to Christianity has passed, and all the Pine Ridge Indians profess belief in Christianity and nominal membership in some church. All but a few of the very oldest people . . . have attended school where religious education was conducted by local missionaries. . . . The Indians now accept most of the principles of Christianity, the ritual, and the sacred calendar (1946: 93).

Feraca (1963) also points out that, despite the rural isolation of traditional Lakota, the reservations were very open to proselytizing, and the impact of Christianity on native life has been deeply felt.

Although a popular notion exists that Catholic missionaries were cruel and patronizing to the Indians, there is also clear evidence that the church in general and the clergy in particular devoted great efforts toward assisting the Sioux during the most harrowing period in their history. Although their intention may have been religious conversion, the Catholic church set up schools and child-care facilities and programs. It assisted families economically and fed huge numbers of people during a period of rationing. It also recorded the native language, writing grammars and dictionaries and ultimately publishing the Bible in Lakota in an all-out effort to persuade the Indian people to become Christians. It was not uncommon for individual missionaries to dedicate their entire lives to the Indians as well as to the church. One of the services provided by the church was room and board in the mission facilities. In the St. Francis Mission at Rosebud, hundreds of Indian children were housed, clothed, fed, and educated. It is not surprising that a tradition has developed of young Indian men becoming priests (Episcopal) or working for the church as teachers, counselors, and guides. The St. Francis Mission School was an important state-approved facility that received federal support from the BIA and, until recently, had boarding facilities. Today the school is totally Indian-controlled and is now known as the St. Francis Indian School. The church's literary achievements continue to play an important role in the development of culturally relevant educational programs. The Mission has developed bilingual curricula using native legends, stories, and myth, and published a Lakota primer in 1973 (*Lakota Woonspe Wowapi*), which is used for native language instruction. The St. Francis Indian School remains the *only* school on the reservation that has a bilingual program.

Many Christian religious practitioners have made efforts to incorporate aspects of the native culture into their worship services. It is common for a church service to contain Lakota prayers and hymns and, not infrequently, sermons. Figures 8 and 9 illustrate the total incorporation of Lakota into parts of the church service. Churches are decorated with native craft work and beaded geometric designs on altar cloths, prayer book covers, and vestments. Currently, elements of Lakota religion are also incorporated into the church service, such as the use of the sacred pipe. This is extremely controversial and has generated both hostility and resentment as well as favorable acceptance among some Lakota. Many Indian people feel that the use of the pipe in the church is sacrilegious and will have disastrous consequences for the church and its Indian members or, worse yet, for the entire reservation community.

Psalm 23. *Dominus regit me.*

1 The LORD is my shepherd;* therefore can I lack nothing.

2 He shall feed me in a green pasture,* and lead me forth beside the waters of comfort.

3 He shall convert my soul,* and bring me forth in the paths of righteousness for his Name's sake.

4 Yea, though I walk through the valley of the shadow of death, I will fear no evil;* for thou art with me; thy rod and thy staff comfort me.

5 Thou shalt prepare a table before me in the presence of them that trouble me;* thou hast anointed my head with oil, and my cup shall be full.

6 Surely thy loving-kindness and mercy shall follow me all the days of my life;* and I will dwell in the house of the LORD for ever.

Psalm 23. *Dominus regit me.*

1 Waawanyaka mitawa kin, ITANCAN kin hee;* wimakakijin kte śni.

2 Peji owiȟankiye en wiȟanmakiya;* wooziiciye mini kin icakda yus-amayan ece.

3 Iye minagi kin yuecetu;* wicoowotanna canku kin okna amayan, iye Caje kin on.

4 Ho, wiconte ohanzi kaksiza kin okna mawani eśa, taku śica wanjina kowakipin kte śni,* niye mici yaun kin heon; cansakana qa cansagye nitawu kin; hena micanptapi.

5 Mitokam waknawotapi wan miyeciknaka, tokamayanpi kin wicitokam;* wikdi on pa sdamayakiya, wiyatke mitawa kin iyatakde.

6 Awicakehan anpetu tona wani kin owasin wowaśte qa wocantkiyewaśte ko miyakna un kta,* qa ITANCAN ti kin anpetu ohinniyan en ounwayin kta.

Figure 8. Lakota–English Psalm (South Dakota Obaspe 1962)

𝕹ational 𝕱estivals — Oyate Tokiksuye Aŋpetu.

108 "God Bless Our Native Land." 6s. 4s.

"Oyate waŋ Itaŋcaŋ kiŋ he Wakaŋtaŋkayapi kiŋ he wowašte yu-
lapi." — Ps. xxxiii: 12.

AMERICA.

1. Wa-kaŋ-taŋ-ka wa-šte, Uŋ-ki-ta-ma-ka-pi Ya-wa-šte ye! He o-i-ca-mna qed Qa o-kpa-za na-kuŋ, Su-ta-ye ḣeiŋ hiŋ kta, Haŋ, o-hiŋ-ni. A-MEN.

From "Goodrich and Gilbert Hymnal" by permission of E. P. Dutton & Co.

2 Tateyaŋpa ḣca ša
Tate qa taja ed
　Initaŋcaŋ,
Nitowašake oŋ
Uŋkitamakapi
Teuŋḣidapi kiŋ,
　Taŋyaŋ hiŋ niŋ.

3 Uŋkitamakapi
Oŋ ceuŋkiyapi;
　Wakaŋtaŋka
Vaŋkaŋd maḣpiya kiŋ

Akotaŋhaŋ yaŋke
Ciŋ He Iye ḣca E
　Uŋkapepi.

4 Uŋkikiyena ḣeiŋ
Yauŋ kiŋ, ohiŋni,
　Awaŋyag uŋ,
Qa ed oyate kiŋ
Niwicayayiŋ kta
Iyonicipi nuŋ,
　Wakaŋtaŋka! AMEN.

Figure 9. Lakota Hymn (South Dakota Obaspe 1962)

The important role that the church occupies in modern Lakota life cannot be underestimated. Most Indian families own Bibles, hymnals, and prayer books. Often a crucifix and pictures of Christ are prominently displayed. Some traditional elderly individuals play church music on the organ and provide musical accompaniment for Sunday services. Hymns are considered especially beautiful when sung in Lakota and are often taped for pleasurable listening at home.

Priests and ministers are almost always called upon to perform baptisms, weddings, and funerals. They stage church retreats to which many people go on weekends. They are respected counselors, and are consulted with freely during periods of familial stress. Clergymen are especially resourceful in assisting families when arrangements are made for funerals and wakes. Often they are the only nonrelatives to spend a full night mourning with a family. It is common practice for such clergymen to offer speeches and prayers on behalf of the deceased at commemorative affairs such as Giveaways.

It is common for the non-Indian outsider to regard Christianity as alien to the Indian. But, in fact, nearly all Lakota are Christians, even those who are also active in native ritual. For the Indian people themselves, the church is an integral and important institution in Lakota society.

7/Language and bilingualism

7.1 NATIVE LANGUAGE MAINTENANCE

Much of the social and cultural life at Rosebud consists of types of activities in which all Lakota (and non-Indians) can participate. However, there is a segment—and quality—of Lakota life that is accessible only to native speakers and those with knowledge of native tradition. Life for these individuals is a totally different experience than for a non-native speaker. It is not so much a question of whether or not a person is fluent in the native language. For the native speaker, life—whether daily routines or participation in traditional affairs—takes on a different quality and has a different set of priorities than for the Lakota that only speak English. In the same manner that a traditional language and lifestyle unify one segment of the reservation population, lack of access to traditional life because of a lack of knowledge of the native language widens the gulf between traditional and assimilated, and permanently separates children from the elderly, the roots of traditionalism.

Maintenance of the native language has always been and continues to be the tie that binds modern Indians to their culture of a century ago. The link is not the result of a conscious attempt to preserve the native language, but is the result of growing up in a traditional community, in a family where the primary language and concerns are Lakota. These Lakota live a lifestyle not so different from their ancestors, despite the fact that they live in commercially manufactured homes and wear store-bought clothes. The way they view the world and the way they interpret life's events reflect a distinct set of perceptions, largely shaped by the language they speak.

Elsewhere on the reservation the native language is rarely heard and native cultural events are virtually absent. These Lakota still enjoy participation in community functions, but their understanding of events that are rooted in indigenous tradition is marginal, their interest more casual, and their participation is only occasional. They cannot initiate, observe, or fully appreciate the types of activities that traditional Lakota are continually involved in because they lack the key that unlocks the world of the nineteenth-century Lakota—knowledge of the native language. This segment of the population relies less on traditional interpretations of events; their thinking and perceptions more closely resemble those of the non-Indian world.

Using knowledge of the native language as a guide, it is easy for the outsider to classify one part of the reservation as traditionally Lakota and the other as assimilating. After all, some communities have mostly native speakers and others consist primarily of English speakers. As opposite ends of a continuum, this is an accurate characterization. But as a description of typical reservation life, it is not meaningful. As with the discussion of community life, it is the overall reservation diversity rather than community uniformity in language use that truly characterizes contemporary Indian life. Lakota at Rosebud range all over this imaginary language continuum.

Most native Lakota speakers are also fluent in English, although the reverse is not true. Native English speakers rarely gain fluency in Lakota, although continuing efforts are made in the schools to teach the Lakota language as a foreign or second language to Indian children who do not speak Lakota. A few elderly traditional Lakota do not speak sufficient English to depend on it, but rely on their adult children to manage transactions that require English competence. This is rare, however; nearly everyone on the reservation speaks English today.

Although more and more Indians at Rosebud are coming to depend on English, it is interesting to note that, for the present, English does *not* seem to be universally replacing the native language on the reservation. English does provide a communication channel for interaction between Indians and non-Indians. But for many Indian people whose daily lives are shaped by a traditional world view and whose daily activities are interspersed with traditional beliefs, rituals, and explanations, the native language uniquely reflects, codes, and expresses *all* of native culture in a way that English cannot.

When two languages survive alongside each other in a single community, the members of the community are considered "functionally bilingual" (Fishman 1972). This term designates a situation in which two languages are used simultaneously in a single speech community, with each language appropriate and therefore reserved for different and specific contexts. As long as a community is functionally bilingual—that is, as long as the Lakota language is necessary for or required in certain social or religious situations—use of the language will persist, if only for those contexts. Dangers of total linguistic assimilation and obsolescence of the native language are likely only in the event that elements of the traditional culture begin to diminish in importance in Lakota life. At the moment this is not occurring, but it is entirely possible that it will. As more and more intermarriage with non-Indians occurs, and as children become more educated in the western sense, the Lakota language is likely to decline in use. Efforts are being made to preserve both the language and the religion. But whether or not such efforts will be sufficient to prevent the death of a language and tradition remains to be seen.

As in the past, Lakota is still the necessary language for participation in all indigenous religious affairs. Participation in traditional religious events is based on interpretations of the Lakota cosmology, and therefore the events only make sense when they are conducted in the native language. The survival of Lakota knowledge, world view, and religion and the concomitant survival of the native language go hand in hand. Persistence of tradition requires that the native language be retained to express it. By the same token, death of native tradition would spell doom for the native language.

As discussed in Chapter 4, some communities such as Spring Creek consist entirely of native speakers; so, for them, *most* routine interaction is characterized by native language use. But for religious affairs, use of Lakota is preferable. In communities such as Antelope, where only half the population can speak Lakota, the same still holds true. People may choose to converse in English or Lakota, but when it comes time for participation in traditional or sacred affairs, they too rely heavily on Lakota. Non-native speakers generally do not participate in indigenous ritual practices, so their lack of knowledge of the native language does not affect the unwritten rule that Lakota is the only language appropriate in religious contexts.

The question of what language is used on what occasions can best be summarized in the following manner. First, native English speakers have no choice: at Rosebud, they are rarely bilingual. Lakota speakers, on the other hand, are nearly always bilingual and so have to decide what language to speak on what occasions. For the traditional Lakota, the choice is self-evident: when at home, with friends or family, Lakota is spoken. When they leave the community to go into town for food, supplies, or business, it is necessary to speak English. Upon occasion, such as when a Spring Creek resident goes to a local store in another community, it is possible to communicate with the clerk in Lakota, *if* both parties know each other and *if* each knows that the other is a native speaker. In this case, the conversation might be predominantly in Lakota. But most stores on the reservation are non-Indian owned, and are staffed with non-Indian (or "half-breed") personnel; and the patron, rather than risk the embarrassment that would result if the clerk did not understand Lakota, depends on English to obtain needed goods.

The same principle applies when a native speaker goes to the town of Rosebud on tribal or BIA business: the employee might or might not be a native speaker. If the two conversants know each other and they know that the other speaks Lakota, the conversation will be in that language. If they are strangers, English is a safer bet.

The only occasion in which Lakota is *spontaneously* spoken in public places is when two very elderly individuals meet for the first time. Since all Lakota over sixty were born in the early 1900s, it is highly unlikely that they would not be totally fluent in the native language. Most people assume this, so elderly people feel secure in addressing other elderly individuals in the native language.

Reliance on the native language in religious contexts is the only occasion in which it is the activities rather than the participants that determine language use. This is not to say that English is *never* spoken at native affairs. In cases where a mixed-blood non-Lakota speaker sponsors a *lowanpi* meeting, some of the conversation between medicine man and sponsor would necessarily be in English. But most non-Lakota speakers are also likely not to be observers of native tradition, although today this is changing. The *yuwipi* or *lowanpi* ceremonies require that prayers be spoken in the native language for several reasons: First, the spirits and supernatural forces contacted are elements of the Lakota belief system and do not have English equivalents. Second, a meeting can only be successful if all ritual prescriptions are followed carefully and exactly. Deviation from the correct performance of the ritual could result in an unsuccessful ceremony, with the possibility that harm would befall the participants for their lack of care. To avoid such an occurrence, ceremonies are conducted exclusively in Lakota.

Upon the rare occasions in which non-Indians are invited to attend native rituals, guests are instructed not only in appropriate behavior, but are advised to speak certain phrases in Lakota—for example, *mitakuye oyas³in* ("all my relatives")—which they must memorize beforehand and recite at the designated moment. Even *their* participation in native ritual must conform to Lakota traditions if they are to be allowed to attend. Today, this is also beginning to change. As more non-native speakers participate in native ritual, English is beginning to take its place even in these sacred contexts.

Public ceremonial events such as the Sun Dance and, to a lesser extent, socioreligious affairs such as Giveaways are also considered traditional occasions and so are conducted primarily in the native language. At Sun Dances in particular, the presiding medicine men address both the participants and spectators in Lakota. Often speeches are delivered by fine public orators in the native language, for which translations into English may or may not be offered. When they are translated, it is often accompanied by statements of regret that this has to be done because many of the young people cannot understand what is being said. On other occasions, no English translation is offered, leaving the non-Indian spectator in the dark, and leaving the young non-native-speaking Lakota with a feeling of shame or regret for his or her inability to fully participate in the day's activities.

As Giveaways vary in character, so do they vary in the language spoken at them. Often the sponsoring family's knowledge of the native language is the determining factor. The other variable is the reason for the Giveaway. Memorial Giveaways tend to be characterized by the use of the native language because the sponsor is more likely to be a traditional person who subscribes to the belief that this ceremony should be observed. A family sponsoring a Giveaway for a homecoming queen or powwow dance contest winner is likely to be a more assimilated family whose children are active in school events. They are less likely to be native speakers; consequently, their Giveaways are most often conducted in English. But a traditional family may celebrate a homecoming queen's victory, as a more assimilated family may hold a memorial. So the language spoken really depends on the individual family.

Although the social context is an important factor in understanding why people prefer to speak one language over another, language choice depends, to a great extent, on the individuals. The general rule is that native speakers prefer to speak their native language when they can. When this is not possible, they resort to English.

Throughout the reservation, it is the elderly who have the greatest native fluency. This seems to be the case regardless of the community in which they live. There is much greater variation for those ranging from the young adult to the middle-aged. Here, the community one comes from on the reservation *is* an important determining factor, for the experiences in each type of community vary considerably. In this age group, it would be safe to estimate that roughly half have native fluency—for although in the traditional villages native fluency is assumed, the number of native speakers in modern communities is much lower. Children and teenagers, as might be expected, make up the group with the fewest Lakota speakers. In places like Spring Creek where children are raised by native speakers (parents or grandparents) and where young people spend most of their free time with other native speakers, their fluency in Lakota is secure. But in Antelope and other communities where there are fewer adult Lakota speakers and where children spend most of their free time in or near a town and school, the number of native speakers drops radically.

If approximately half of the adult reservation population has any knowledge of the native language today, and only about one-fourth of young people at Rosebud are native speakers, the obvious question is, what happens when the young people become the adult generation, and the majority of elderly are gone? This question has been a source of much concern—and some worry—for many people, and has become the reason for the strong push to introduce native language programs throughout the reservation's schools. Adults fear that without knowledge of the native language, young people will lose contact with the elderly generation and so will lose the opportunity to learn and appreciate much of the traditional culture. They fear that this process of language loss and cultural deterioration has already begun. They fear that this lack of knowledge has already resulted in the absence of pride in one's "Indianness," an indifference toward the moral values and attitudes revered by the older generations, and, worst of all, the lack of a feeling of belonging in either the native culture or the surrounding non-Indian society. The feeling of marginality breeds resentment in young people and contributes to an already problematic situation: they have little to do, many are not particularly interested in school, and there is tremendous pressure to drink. On top of all this, self-esteem is low. They are an isolated group, economically insecure and slowly losing touch with their native heritage. Whether or not native language programs in the schools will be adequate to halt the process of native language and culture loss will be taken up in the next chapter, which deals with revitalization efforts.

7.2 LINGUISTIC ACCULTURATION

The fact that Rosebud is a bilingual community and that being an English speaker is as typical of the Indian experience as being a Lakota speaker is only one of the many results of linguistic acculturation. The situation is actually far more complex. In all the years during which the two languages (and cultures) have come into contact, certain changes have begun to occur, both in the actual language and in the way English and Lakota have come to be mixed together. In addition, the patterns in speaking English have even been influenced by the native language. All these types of changes are part of the process of linguistic acculturation, the coming into contact of one language by another. The results of this contact are many and varied. First, the most striking observation is that Lakota and English are frequently used together—even within a single utterance. "Bilingual shifting" or "code switching," the alternation between two languages or speech styles, is very characteristic of reservation speech. Second, many aspects of the native language itself have begun to change. New vocabulary to reflect western concepts, technology, and values has been introduced into the native language, creating a new lexicon and a new colloquial style of speaking. Lastly, the English spoken at Rosebud has been influenced by native speech to the extent that it, too, has been locally altered. Each one of these important changes will be discussed separately.

Listening to Lakota in conversation, the most striking characteristic is the continual interjection of English words within an otherwise Lakota sentence. To the outsider this might seem odd—why would a native speaker, if comfortable in his or her own language, need to depend on English at all? Is this evidence of a gradual switch to English? The answer is no. Bilingual shifting has little or nothing to do with the adoption of a new language, but rather is an expression of the fact that *some things,* particularly western things or ideas, are more easily expressed in English. By the same token, other phenomena, such as religious concepts, remain the province of the native language.

The interjection of English words and phrases and especially idiosyncratic expressions into an otherwise Lakota sentence represents a particular kind of linguistic adaptation, and a highly patterned one at that. English words are interjected only when the speaker wants to express a particular idea or concept that is western in origin or that expresses the thought more easily than if a translation were attempted. Since many of the activities in daily life reflect western economy, education, employment, or subsistence, Lakota must incorporate a sufficient amount of English to deal with these subjects effectively without totally sacrificing the use of their native language. The result is a curious-sounding intermixture with few enough English words that a non-Lakota speaker will have real difficulty getting the gist of the conversation.

Of course, Lakota is not always spoken in this mixed fashion. Certainly upon ceremonial occasions, little or no English is interjected, since the subjects being discussed stem largely from native life. But even on these occasions, it is not uncommon to witness the insertion of English words. Most often, Lakota speakers use English to express western divisions of time, quantities, amounts, holidays, school or job activities, and numbers—not because there are no terms for these concepts in the native language, but because the native language expresses them differently. For example, although women sewed clothing during precontact times, they did not purchase fabric in yards and inches—such measurements are western means of referring to units of size. Similarly, we know that Lakota expresses the passing of time in particular ways, but not in hours, minutes, and seconds. Yet modern Lakota must use these concepts and terms in modern-day life, for they too must keep schedules and appointments, must purchase their goods in stores, and must be at work from eight to five. The logical result of the combining of Indian and non-Indian tradition is the combining in languages also.

The second type of linguistic acculturation easily observed is the addition of new words to the Lakota lexicon—words that are English in origin but that have been given Lakota translations. Although any Lakota speaker might prefer to shift into English to express these particular items or concepts, one *can* use the Lakota translation if it is desirable to speak purely in the native language. New vocabulary that regularly appears in Lakota conversation refers to western items such as the following:

English word	Lakota word	Lakota literal translation
dresser	yusluwognaka	"pull and store"
typewriter	wanaȟtagyapi	"make it kick"
automobile	iyečikinyanka	"runs by itself"
clock	mazaškanškan	"iron that moves"
sewing machine	maswičeǧe	"iron that sews"

These English words—dresser, typewriter, automobile, clock, and sewing machine— all reflect western phenomena that *can* be expressed in Lakota without sacrificing precise meaning, although it is my guess that most Lakota referring to these things would be more likely to interject them in their English forms into an otherwise Lakota sentence. But in Lakota curriculum materials and newspapers, of course, the Lakota translation is available and would be preferred.

There is another kind of linguistic acculturation occurring within this second broad category of lexical changes. This involves a shift from the purer, more traditional manner of speaking (*yatʔinsya woglaka,* "to talk firm," referring to the formal style of speaking) to the more modern, casual speech more characteristic of young people (called *ikčeya woglaka,* which means "to talk ordinary"). Today, modern short Lakota words and colloquialisms are substituted for the long, richly expressive ones that used to be typical of the language prior to acculturation. Old people say that the pure and traditional form of their language, sometimes referred to as "slow speech," is gradually falling into obsolescence because the younger generation does not know or take the time to learn the old words or expressions for things. They take shortcuts and use slang or "fast speech," and rely on a Lakota that, the elderly say, is briefer, less rich in its visual referents, and is not aesthetically beautiful. For example, the modern Lakota word for tobacco is *cunšaša*—literally "willow." But in the old days the proper term was *zintkalatȟačanliʔičahiye*—which, when broken down, refers to a description of small birds perching on a river locust; this plant, when mixed together with other tobaccos or herbs, creates a mixture for smoking in the sacred pipe. Another example is the Lakota term for "silhouetted," now in colloquial speech *najin.* But in the formal, proper way of speaking, the term *amaȟposantagliya* is preferred, conjuring up images of a person riding on horseback set against the background of the sky. (For a more detailed discussion of this topic, see Taylor and Rood 1972; Grobsmith 1979b.)

Why have these terms begun to fall into obsolescence? Just as new western concepts must be newly created and expressed in English, so old Lakota expressions begin to lose their meanings as fewer ties remain to the culture of a century ago. The loss of this old variety of speaking is not without regret for the elderly, who find their children's speech to be crude, colloquial in nature, and too much like American slang. The elders say of their children:

> These kids are in too much of a hurry. . . . They don't take time to learn how to talk good. . . . They just say anything.

The way in which the use of English has begun to alter native speech is the third type of linguistic acculturation common at Rosebud. Most Lakota who speak English speak a variety of English that, technically, is known as nonstandard English (NSE). Throughout the United States, types of NSE vary with the region, ethnic population, and degree of tie with the native language. Nonstandard English at Rosebud is influenced most heavily by Lakota grammar, such as in the area of syntax or word order, and phonology, which affects the production of English sounds.

Even the use of nonstandard English varies at Rosebud, depending on the community from which one comes or on one's individual life circumstances. Elderly or full-blooded Indians who have seldom left the reservation in their lifetimes speak a style of NSE that resembles their native language most closely. They speak English with a Lakota accent, and use grammatical constructs that more closely resemble the native language than they do English. Such things as tense and plural markers differ for English and Lakota, but a Lakota speaker who knows little English may create a plural or a tense using the Lakota rule for an English construct. The result is a sentence like the following:

> Long time ago when we talk Indian they wash our mouth out with soap and make us sit in a corner.

Here, the elimination of past tense in English shows the influence of Lakota rules of agreement. Rules of syntax also differ for the two languages. In English, we place adjectives before nouns, but in Lakota, adjectives generally follow nouns, resulting in expressions like "button belly" and "bear black" instead of "belly button" or "black bear."

Lakota who are more familiar with English, either from being in the military service or living off-reservation for a time, generally are more familiar with English grammatical construction and speak a variety of NSE that differs from the standard variety only in that it is heavily influenced by Lakota phonology or pronunciation. Today, young Indian people who grow up speaking English in their homes or who continue their education beyond high school speak a variety of English indistinguishable from the surrounding non-Indian community. This style is generally characteristic of lower socioeconomic groups in urban areas, rural farmers, ranchers, and with groups having little exposure to formal education.

As the above discussion illustrates, speech at Rosebud is not a simple matter of Lakota versus English. As the two languages meet, each begins to undergo certain changes, sometimes permanently. But despite the changes that each undergoes and the continuing influence of one upon the other, they remain distinct and do not replace one another as might be assumed. It is easy for the outsider to assume that since today's Lakota must live in the modern world, their language ought to be relinquished and should give way to the dominant's society's language, for success in education and employment depend, for the most part, on one's competence in English. There are Indian people who feel this way, too—they see their language as being obsolete and unnecessary to contemporary survival. But people who feel this way are in the minority; the majority of Lakota continue to depend on their native language, if not all the time, for specific occasions for which English substitutes are simply unacceptable. And, for the moment, it is safe to say that Lakota is not yet a dying language.

8/Cultural revitalization and
the school

8.1 BILINGUAL PROGRAMS AND
NATIVE LANGUAGE INSTRUCTION

The kinds of linguistic acculturation occurring at Rosebud, which have been discussed in the previous chapter, indicate that although at present the native language does not appear to be becoming obsolete, there is generally an increasing uneasiness at Rosebud about loss of this most basic link to the traditional culture. Also discussed in the last chapter was the linguistic heterogeneity of the reservation and how the native language was alive and well in some communities (Spring Creek, for example), slowly disappearing at others (like Antelope), and virtually absent at still others. Although there are some Indian people who would just as soon see Lakota fade into the past, the majority of Lakota *are* beginning to be concerned over the possible extinction of their language and, ultimately, their native culture. For this reason, efforts to bring the native language into the school are being made in an attempt to arrest the process of linguistic obsolescence. Whether these efforts at revitalization will be successful or whether they reflect too little too late can only be determined by time. Considering how few native speakers there are in some communities, the school may represent the only possible forum in which a child *can* become familiar with his or her traditional language. But lacking linguistic reinforcement in the home, there is serious question if any but the most superficial acquaintance with a language can be gained in this manner.

Before taking a close look at language instruction and the feasibility of bilingual programs at Rosebud, it is necessary to point out that the wide range in knowledge of the native language (the reservation heterogeneity that has been discussed) works *against* the incorporation of permanent and meaningful language retention programs. A number of circumstances indicate why this is so. The first consideration is the fact that in communities such as Spring Creek, where nearly everyone, including children, is fluent in Lakota, language retention programs are considered superfluous, unnecessary. Why should a native language program be created for children who are already native speakers? Instruction in the native language is usually part of a broader goal—that of cultural revitalization or a conscious intent on preservation of one's traditions. But this requires that a population feel threatened by and want to ward off assimilation. In the case of Spring Creek, loss of the native culture seems remote, an unreal consideration, and so there is little

96

or no political consciousness about making a concerted effort to preserve this heritage. The second consideration is that even with a community such as Spring Creek, where a genuine bilingual program or curriculum *could* be introduced (since children all speak Lakota), there are not enough trained, competent bilingual teachers who could direct such efforts. So, in the very communities where a truly bilingual curriculum *could* be implemented, it is unlikely to happen. Another consideration is that, in reality, most communities have far fewer native speakers than Spring Creek, so true bilingual instruction—even if there *were* trained and qualified teachers—would still be impossible. And lastly, little emphasis is placed on literacy in the traditional culture, further discouraging the development of bilingual curricula.

Because of these circumstances—unevenness of the school population in their ability to speak the native language, and a lack of trained personnel—true bilingual programs in which children study various school subjects *in* two languages are impossible. The implications of this are great. First, children whose first language is Lakota are not able to use the language they know best in their first experiences at school. This has been cited as one of the main reasons for early disaffection with school and a reduction in the quality of learning for the child. Secondly, these children sometimes resent the fact that their native language is not used in the classroom. They wonder if their language is somehow inadequate for or inappropriate to formal education. This is the beginning of a long process of alienation from school and a child's growing compartmentalization of school and home, an abyss that seldom closes. Lastly, the hasty switch to English (either at Head Start, kindergarten, or first grade) results not only in intellectual alienation for the child, but emotional problems as well. Native-speaking children feel less secure with what is happening around them; they feel isolated, uncertain, and become marginal participants in classroom activities. These responses to early school experiences are less common today than they were for prior generations of Lakota who spoke virtually *no* English prior to coming to school. Today, children even in the traditional villages speak a good deal of English as they begin their first year of school—so this trauma and crisis have been reduced. But these circumstances have in the past and continue in the present to affect the quality of education for nearly all Indian people—and Rosebud is no exception. It is these types of events that account for children's disinterest in school, for the lack of meaning and relevance of school in their lives, and ultimately, for the high dropout rate of Indian high school students.

Efforts at cultural and linguistic revitalization are aimed not only at eliminating these types of conflicts and improving the quality of education for the Lakota child, but also at making the school experience a vital and meaningful one that helps prepare children intellectually and emotionally for life.

Native language instruction programs exist throughout the reservation and are regularly available to Lakota children, whether they speak the native language or not. In these programs, teachers work with native speakers from the various communities to bring the native language into the classroom. For many children, this is their first and perhaps only exposure to the traditional language. Unlike a bilingual program, the instruction process is carried on *in* English, although the *subject* is the Lakota language. The curriculum materials, also, as for any other foreign language study, are written to teach the language to an English-speaking student. Several books are available for this, the most widely used being a book produced and published at the St. Francis Indian School called *Lakota Woonspe Wowapi* (1973). College classes in Lakota depend more heavily on the grammar developed by Taylor and Rood (1972), known as the Colorado Lakota Project. In conjunction with the texts, stories and literature in the native language are available for the student to read and translate.

Students are said to enjoy native language instruction classes, for they are learning, many for the first time, a way to have access to elements of local life previously inaccessible to them. Children exhibit much pride in learning Lakota words and grammar. But whether such programs can truly teach native fluency is certainly open to question. For some students, years of instruction, diligent work, and a real effort to incorporate and apply their newfound skills in the world around them may result in near-native fluency or, at the least, an increase in their understanding and enjoyment of native events. But for the majority of students, language instruction is an isolated class, a formal learning experience not so easily linked to reality. Acquisition of some new vocabulary does certainly lend pride and pleasure, but hopes of gaining native fluency are slim. In this manner, hopes of revitalizing the native language—that is, bringing a language falling into obsolescence back to life—is indeed a remote prospect.

8.2.   NATIVE AMERICAN STUDIES PROGRAMS

Native language instruction is only one part of a larger program whose goal it is to make native life accessible to all Lakota children regardless of their style of life. The Native American or Indian Studies Program provides elementary through high school students with an academic format for the incorporation of native knowledge into an otherwise western school experience. What is the rationale behind such a program and how has it been received by the reservation community? Formal schooling in state-approved schools has been a part of Indian life since the 1870s. For most Native Americans during the first half of the twentieth century, education often meant removal from home, criticism of native life along with punishment for speaking the native language, and an unrelenting effort on the part of the school, its teachers, and administration to replace native values and attitudes with western Christian ideas. Children having little or no knowledge of the English language were taken from their homes and families and were refashioned according to western standards. Boys were taught vocational skills and learned trades, and girls were taught the domestic arts, such as cooking and sewing. If little else was learned, most students understood that being Indian was bad, that native languages were considered primitive, undesirable, and irrelevant, and that conformity to a non-Indian standard was expected. Many adults at Rosebud today speak with great bitterness about their experiences, the beatings they received, and the feelings of shame they suffered. Most adults came out of the experience disliking school and feeling that white man's education was a necessary evil. School did not equip them for life in today's world. It did, however, teach them the lesson that success in America meant education, so now, if for no other reason than that they want their children to be able to get jobs, they promote the notion that school is essential. But for the very traditional Lakota, school is only a means to an end—it is not in *itself* a valuable or meaningful experience. For this reason, their encouragement of children to attend school is less than convincing. One very traditional woman I knew well illustrated this in her actions. One day she went to get her son out of school so that he could help her with the chores—caring for the livestock and so forth. When she got to school, she discovered that her son had played hooky and had not come to school that day at all. She was furious! How dare her son cut classes to fool around! But what she did *not* see was that in her son's experience at home he had learned that school was important because the white man required it, *not* because it was inherently worthwhile. Her son understood that chores and life's everyday tasks *were* indeed basic to survival, but that school was not. Today, he is a high school dropout.

As the field of Indian education develops and as Indian people become more aware of their needs and rights, more emphasis has been placed on the value of being an educated individual *not only* in the white man's world—so one can get a job—but in the Indian world, so one can become a full human being whose identity is secure. In a period of history in which one's ethnic ties and roots are considered an important feature in one's identity and sense of self-worth, the notion of Indian pride has blossomed. The logical outcome and outlet of this newfound sense of pride and integrity is the study of native life, now a standard part of school curricula throughout reservation areas.

Although Native American Studies programs receive wide support throughout Rosebud, it is necessary to mention that not all Lakota adults are in agreement with its philosophy. While in the minority, these individuals are quick to point out that when they went to school, Indian life was a forbidden subject. Its revival—now as a part of the curriculum—is, they fear, a pointless exercise that will help little in their children's effort to get a good education. They believe that students and teachers should concentrate their efforts on preparing Native Americans for jobs by giving them the skills required by today's society. They fear that Indian Studies will focus attention on the historic past rather than the future, and that the study of Indian life is only a fad—and a harmful one at that. It is not difficult to see why they are perplexed and angry that subjects that were once drummed out of their lives should now be a topic for classroom discussion. They want their children to succeed by being competitive in the non-Indian world, and they view Indian Studies as a movement "back to the blanket," back to a past that they feel is better forgotten.

This view is not the typical one at Rosebud. Indian Studies programs have nearly everyone's support. But the view of these classes as pointless exercises is an opinion that must be taken into account. Certainly the children in families with these views feel the impact of their parents' philosophy, for they are forbidden from participating in such classes.

Indian Studies classes offer the Lakota student a variety of native subjects. The events of Indian history and culture are introduced through the use of printed

Lakota students who take Indian Studies in school enjoy their participation in the Todd County parade.

materials such as William Pike's *Indian History and Culture* (1972), a book of sixty-five lessons for "modern Indians." Curriculum materials like these offer lessons in a wide range of topics, such as Indian battles and heroes, the cultures of non-Lakota Plains tribes, Sioux religion, and Indian values. In addition to these traditional subjects, Indian Studies also offers students the opportunity to study, design, and make costumes of native dress, which are proudly displayed during such events as the Todd County Indian Studies Parade, an annual event in Mission. Native crafts are especially popular, for beadwork and quillwork are still worn at powwows, and children proudly display the products of their labor. Since the Lakota never made pottery or basketry, Indian arts and crafts emphasize traditional skills such as beading and quillwork and a contemporary expression of Indian symbols and design in the area of drawing and painting. In the last few years, local artists have been praised for their contribution to the expression of Indian pride, and children today emulate them and strive to develop similar talents. The results have been remarkable. Not only is there a new role for children to observe, but painting and design have become modern vehicles to communicate Indian heritage and pride. Annual fairs and exhibits display the work of children and local artists alike and some exhibits, such as the one at Holy Rosary Mission on the neighboring Pine Ridge Reservation, have developed national reputations.

Indian Studies classes rely not only on trained staff and instructors, but depend on the participation of elderly or traditional individuals in the community, who are brought in to share their knowledge with the classes. Lakota music, dance, drumming, and singing are subjects deeply enjoyed by the young, for all are expressed in local events such as the powwow and Giveaway, as well as ceremonies such as the Sun Dance. Knowledge of native music and dance enhances children's enjoyment of and participation in these events, although it is not likely that many of these skills are truly gained in the classroom. Most Lakota children learn the meaning of these activities by attending social affairs from their infancy on. The children who are *not* familiar with Lakota music and dance from personal experience are also less likely to be permitted by their parents to take Indian Studies in school. So the real benefit derived from such occasions is not so much gaining the actual skill as it is communicating to the child that knowledge of these subjects is valuable and important. The pleasure and the pride derived from giving Lakota subjects a place in the otherwise western school curriculum has changed some children's opinion of even going to school, and has rendered the native subjects more "legitimate."

Lakota or Indian Studies is not restricted to grade school or high school. Programs focusing on Native American life are also offered at the college level at the local Sinte Gleska (Spotted Tail) Community College, which offers specializations in several fields, one of which is Lakota studies. A student can pursue an Associate of Arts Degree in Indian Studies, and can choose to specialize further, selecting one of three areas of emphasis: Lakota (Sioux) history and culture, Lakota language, or Lakota traditional arts.

8.3   COLLEGE PROGRAMS

It is rare that Native Americans have an opportunity to pursue a college education while remaining on their home reservation because few colleges exist in reservation communities throughout the United States. Having the opportunity to attend college without having to leave home is an unfulfilled dream for most Indian people. At Rosebud as well as Pine Ridge this dream has become a reality and today, many Lakota take courses, either pursuing an associate of arts degree or a bachelor's degree (the college began as a junior college but now offers a four-year program.) The establishment of this institution relieved Indian people of what had been a difficult decision for generations: to remain uneducated in their home communities, or to leave friends and relatives in pursuit of advanced education. For the Lakota at Rosebud, as on most reservations, the difficulties inherent in leaving home and relocating in a city where there was a college were so great that, historically, few have chosen to do it. Relocating meant leaving dependent children at home, or having to arrange for child care on a daily basis, which few could afford. (At Rosebud, grandparents often care for small children while parents are at work, thereby eliminating babysitting costs.) Relocating meant expenses in food, housing, and fuel that were far greater than at home. The expense of travel alone seemed formidable. Because most Lakota marry and begin their families at a relatively young age, they are less likely to be free of financial and social obligations and able to go to college. Although financial assistance for college has been available through the Bureau of Indian Affairs, the difficulties of moving one's family—or leaving them—have prevented or discouraged Indian people from seeking higher education.

The founding of Sinte Gleska College in 1971 meant, for the Lakota, a new opportunity to gain the education or training they desired without having to sacrifice life at home. Now it was possible to attend classes, obtain college credits, and receive a two-year certificate or diploma while remaining in an environment that provided them with security, stability, and emotional support. Going to college at home also eliminated the culture shock Indian people undergo when they relocate to urban areas, a situation that all too often results in their intense loneliness and isolation and eventual return to the reservation. The college is not by any means a panacea for the ills of unemployment, the lack of jobs at Rosebud, and the problems of gaining college training, but it is a major step in the direction of improvement and development of opportunity.

Sinte Gleska College began as a result of a community desire for both local education and local control. The roots and origins of the college lie in the philosophy of self-determination—the desire to plan for and meet the communities' needs. The founders of the college expressed a desire to provide education and opportunities derived from *having* an education to their children. In a pamphlet describing the college, the needs of the people are clearly stated:

> Too often they had seen young people leave for college and soon return home frustrated and defeated. The Board . . . wishes to offer quality education . . . such that they [Indian people] can succeed in the Indian and non-Indian world. . . . The Indian student should have the skills intellectually, interpersonally and technically to succeed. The Sinte Gleska College is to be the mechanism by which the Indian person can gain these skills.

(Sinte Gleska Community College pamphlet)

In 1966 and 1967, discussions about implementing these goals began. By 1969, the reservation community had brought a resolution to the Rosebud Sioux Tribal Council advocating the establishment of the college. The resolution passed unanimously. In 1970, plans for funding were drawn up. The college opened in February 1971 as a chartered institution of higher education incorporated in the State of South Dakota as a nonprofit organization. Today, the college is controlled by an all-Indian Board of Regents that works in an effort to coordinate the community's needs for both adult education as well as accredited college-level classes.

Today, the college is officially a recognized candidate for accreditation through the North Central Association of Colleges and Universities. However, the college has formed a unique relationship with Black Hills State College in Spearfish, South Dakota, and the University of South Dakota at Vermillion and Springfield, to which credits may be transferred to obtain a college diploma. Courses offered by the college have comparable counterparts at Black Hills State and the University of South Dakota, so that Lakota taking classes at Sinte Gleska are able to transfer their credits to these schools and can apply for a transfer of credits at other institutions as well. But both the associate degree and the bachelor's degree from the college are recognized as valid degrees of the two associated institutions. (Gerald Mohatt, personal communication)

When the college first opened, courses were taught by volunteer instructors.

Today, instructors generally have advanced degrees as well as specialized training and skills in their areas of expertise. Although the college makes an effort to hire Lakota to fill faculty and staff positions, non-Indians are employed as well. Students at the college number several hundred and the college maintains a sizeable enrollment, a reflection of the popularity and success of the college with the people. The college has now been in operation for nearly a decade, and it continues to expand in efforts to meet the needs of the Lakota at Rosebud. Today, the college offers the associate of arts degree in the following fields: education, business, general studies, human services, Lakota or Indian studies, and nursing; there are also nondegree programs and two bachelor's degrees—in human services and in education.

Students of the college can receive financial support in the form of BIA scholarships and tuition waivers if they are one-fourth Lakota or more and are enrolled members of the Rosebud Sioux tribe. Expense grants such as BEOG (Basic Educational Opportunity Grants) are available for up to eight semesters of undergraduate work. Eligibility for BEOG is based on income. College classes are open to anyone wishing to attend, including non-Indians living in the reservation area.

One of the reasons for the college's growth and popularity is that classes are offered to community members in numerous locations throughout the reservation rather than just at the college center. For many, the convenience of this "dispersed model" makes all the difference between attending college or not. Schoolteachers or teacher aides can take a college course in the afternoon or evening after they are finished teaching school for the day. If they have no car, it is no problem: the college sends the instructor and the course to them! Wherever there is a need or demand, the college arranges courses to accommodate Lakota in all the outlying communities where courses would benefit a group of people. The college emphasizes this attitude in their philosophy—that education must be made available to all Lakota, whether or not they can afford transportation, child care, or books. Many employed adults earn college credits that lead toward advanced degrees or provide them with sufficient hours and training to make them eligible for state-controlled raises.

But, like everything else, the college, too, suffers certain problems. Financial needs continue to grow and the college suffers chronically from inadequate funding, sometimes resulting in cuts that eliminate staff and parts of programs. Salaries for instructors are barely competitive with colleges and universities outside the reservation, making it difficult to attract fine teachers. And, like every political and educational institution, Sinte Gleska, too, suffers from internal strife, factionalism among the Indian people, difficulties concerning control and autonomy, and other problems characteristic of such organizations. But Sinte Gleska has a set of problems that are unique to the field of Indian education as a whole—that of providing quality education to the individuals who have had poor high school training or an inadequate background in study and reading skills. Some students either do poorly or college standards must be lowered to allow them to succeed. Since this is a problem of all Indian schools, it will be discussed in the next section on conflicts of cultures and cultural styles in the classroom.

8.4 CULTURAL STYLES OF LEARNING

Despite advances in the field of education and especially Native American education, the classroom experience continues to present a series of challenges—both for the teacher and the Lakota child (or adult student)—that are unique to reservation schools. Unlike public schools in urban areas where the majority of pupils and teachers share a common cultural background, a reservation Indian child is nearly always in a class planned and taught by a non-Indian teacher. The cultural gap is often bridged today by the use of Lakota teacher aides, who can more effectively manage a situation in which a Lakota child has a problem rooted in language or cultural style. But the majority of teachers today are non-Indian and this immediately poses certain problems.

Most schoolteachers on the reservation come from areas quite far from Rosebud. They are from cities in South Dakota or other states, with only a few coming from the reservation proper. When they arrive at Rosebud, they are confronted with a culture foreign to them. To begin with, teachers are housed in a compound or housing area restricted to state or federal employees, so immediately they are isolated from the reservation population. Not only are they set apart physically, but in the Indian view they are also separated socially and symbolically. The teachers themselves feel that they are separate; few socialize with Indian people, most preferring the comfort and familiarity of visiting with other non-Indians. The chasm between Indian and non-Indian is widened by this social isolation, both by the difference in quality of housing between Indians and whites and the separation in activity. Confronted with loneliness, social isolation, and an inability to integrate themselves fully into the Indian community, they pull up stakes after a year or two and move on.

It is necessary to consider why non-Indian teachers move to reservation areas to teach. Some feel that teaching in a school where children are predominantly of a culture different from their own poses a new and interesting challenge and a life experience from which they can learn and benefit. Others enter a reservation community with feelings of wanting to save, missionize, or westernize Indian children. And still others seek employment in isolated reservation areas to get away from other pressures, and come to the reservation ill-prepared for the set of challenges they will face. Some meet the challenges, socially and educationally. They adjust. Others struggle and fail.

The majority of teachers are aware that teaching in a cross-cultural classroom presents a unique set of circumstances and problems, but few are trained or prepared to deal with them effectively. Historically, the result has been failure—for both the teacher and the child. The high turnover of teachers in reservation schools is evidence of the stress and difficulty a non-Indian teacher faces. In the State of South Dakota, teachers are now required to take three hours of Indian studies. This recent policy has been designed to help teachers familiarize themselves with the specific history, language, and culture of the children they will teach. Since many Lakota children do not come from extremely traditional families, a lack of knowledge of specific traditions is not so critical. But many teachers lack knowledge and experience in teaching children who come from poor families, perhaps with crowded homes, no indoor plumbing, perhaps with elderly, ill, or alcoholic parents. The living conditions for the Indian child are rarely what the non-Indian teacher has assumed; children may have little or no room to work at home, and rarely have their own room or desk or even a place to do their schoolwork. At home, children face everyday experiences that, although they do not directly relate to the children's education, cannot help but affect it. A student with alcoholic brothers and sisters may face daily fights and arguments, sometimes even brutal experiences with death. If the student has alcoholic parents, he or she may become a surrogate parent and care for the younger children, even on an almost permanent basis. Sometimes, Indian homes are so crowded that a child feels driven to wander around and hang out with friends rather than endure the depressing environment of poverty and crowding.

Of course, not all children experience such difficult times. But it is common for every Lakota child to experience some of these things at least part of the time. If these types of events are outside the realm of the teacher's ordinary, everyday experience, the teacher may not recognize or be able to help the children who are burdened before they even walk into the classroom each morning.

Aside from the direct pressures, there are other situations that teachers may not realize affect their students' involvement, or lack of it, in their schoolwork. One of these is the lack of reading materials and the lack of general exposure to written materials that is characteristic of most Indian homes. Coming from a nonliterate tradition, few Lakota receive newspapers or magazines. Where the average non-Indian child becomes familiar with these types of publications—if only to determine television and movie schedules—the Indian child remains unfamiliar with such reading materials. Because Lakota come from an oral tradition, where word-of-mouth was the way most information was communicated, children do not depend on books and magazines as do non-Indian children, and therefore do not develop reading skills. And, unlike most non-Indian homes, rarely are there areas in the home furnished with lamps and designated as reading areas. So the traditional culture, an oral or nonliterate one, does encourage children to explore one channel of learning and communication, but this is *not* the one that is assumed in the classroom. Teachers often assume, erroneously, that the home environment is supportive of the Indian child's school experience, when, in reality, the two circumstances have little bearing on one another.

Aside from these indirect problems, there is yet a third type of situation that further inhibits success in the classroom. This is actual conflict in cultural style, the result of two different value systems coming together in an environment that is just beginning to recognize, appreciate, and make use of these differences.

Indian children are often taught different sets of rules, values, and traditions from non-Indian children. Some of these differences are known to teachers, but, for the most part, they are a mysterious source of conflict between teacher and child. Lakota society teaches young people to honor solidarity and friendship beyond all other things, and the result of this closeness among young people is heavy pressure to conform to the behavior of one's peer group. Whether this involves drinking, joyriding, or simply not tattling on one's friends, the result is often the same for the teacher—confrontation with a united front of tight-lipped children. It would be incorrect to say that the traditional culture teaches children to be noncompetitive, as has been generalized for many Native American peoples; but, it is true that native culture values humility and modesty to the extent that putting effort into outdoing one's peers is strictly inappropriate. Teachers wonder sometimes why students are unresponsive, but insight into Lakota values illustrates that if one person fails to know the answer to a question, for another to show off and excel in the face of his or her friend's failure is undignified behavior and is simply not done. Because of this traditional rejection by children of individualism, especially when pursuit of it would make one's friends look bad, teachers who persist in using an individual approach to classroom instruction may find that they meet with repeated failure.

In recent years, teachers and administrators have become increasingly aware of cross-cultural problems and have made efforts to educate teachers not so much in traditional subjects (native history and so on), but in traditional values and manners. Workshops are occasionally offered by the school in which teachers meet with trained personnel—educators, linguists, and anthropologists—to learn teaching techniques that are not culturally bound or culture-specific. For example, a teacher might be encouraged to elicit a response from students by trying a choral response, that is, a group response, rather than singling out and embarrassing students. This type of experiment is very important, because continuing the old pattern of "teacher demanding, student not responding" becomes a nonproductive and unhappy interaction that does *anything* but reinforce a good attitude toward school. It is far too early to tell whether sufficient efforts will be made to inform and train teachers in new skills, as educators learn more about cross-cultural problems and techniques of overcoming them, but one thing is certain: without such efforts, patterns of classroom interaction are likely to persist that result in student failure, teacher frustration, and a high dropout rate—for both teacher and pupil.

9/Contemporary Rosebud

9.1 POLITICS ON THE RESERVATION

Ever since the 1973 occupation of Wounded Knee, most of the Sioux have gained a wider national reputation than they had enjoyed before. Perhaps until that time, most Americans believed that Indian cultures still existed as small and insignificant ethnic clusters scattered throughout America's wastelands. After the 1973 occupation, the plight of the Sioux—and of all Native Americans, for that matter—was brought to the attention of the public. A poor standard of living, substandard housing, oppression by the federal government, and corruption of local political organizations combined to set off a cry of frustration that was heard nationwide. For many Oglala at Pine Ridge, the outcry was one with which they were deeply sympathetic. But for the Brule at Rosebud, a deep fear and suspicion grew about the members of the organization that formed and carried out the protest at Wounded Knee—the American Indian Movement (AIM).

This organization was founded in 1968 by several Indian leaders from Minnesota who were concerned about Indian rights, especially in off-reservation areas. In the first few years of its existence, it developed a reputation for its militant nature, for it represented an attitude about effecting social change through use of active and aggressive techniques rather than passive acceptance of the status quo. AIM organized chapters throughout the United States to deal with issues such as racial prejudice, political negligence, and violence against Native Americans, and their methods sometimes involved confrontation, occupation, and the use of weapons. The other important feature of AIM's philosophy was an appreciation of native tradition and the desire to incorporate, when possible, elements of indigenous life into modern living. In this way, AIM has become affiliated with a revival in religion, native rituals, foods, and customs. Traditional medicine men, both at Rosebud and Pine Ridge, act as sponsors who provide spiritual guidance to its members. AIM has come to be associated with native revitalization because, regardless of one's tribal affiliation, it supports a view of an appreciation of, if not a return to, native life. The philosophy of AIM is one of taking pride in one's Indian identity and behaving with integrity. Not only does the organization encourage individual pride, but they have emphasized the importance of tribal and intertribal solidarity. Their public statement of the need for a resurgence in Indian pride has caused a reawakening—both political and cultural—throughout the United States in gen-

107

eral and in South Dakota in particular. The strong presence and participation of AIM in the 1972 Sun Dance at Pine Ridge has stood as a statement of Indian brotherhood and the continuing viability of Indian values. But, for many Lakota, AIM's two values of militancy and traditionalism are diametrically opposed.

In the last decade, AIM has come to represent the politically radical, the hostile, and, as an association of people with shared interests, has become more separate, unified, and self-contained. Conducting their own ceremonies, which are sometimes closed to non-Indians, they have come to be considered a strong political force to be reckoned with.

Although there is an AIM chapter at Rosebud that is active and enjoys a substantial membership, many Lakota at Rosebud find this force frightening and menacing. Some communities at Rosebud have a greater degree of involvement in and sympathy with AIM activities than do others. More conservative villages tend to regard militant sympathies as being characteristically un-Indian. They disapprove of AIM's activities, fear possible violent outbursts, and reject any association with the organization. When militants appear at local powwows or Giveaways, there is much gossip and criticism, but, in the typically Lakota fashion, their presence is tolerated. During the summer of 1974, while I was living at Rosebud, an episode involving AIM members occurred at a local country club that resulted in injury to several individuals. People on the reservation seemed deeply disturbed by this, and feared further outbreaks of violence that could potentially bring harm to them, their families, and property. Although AIM members claimed that the skirmish involved standing up for Indian rights, many Lakota people condemned the event. They say that the resolutions AIM seeks for problems go against the peaceful settlement process that, AIM's critics say, is more typically "Indian."

The American Indian Movement's reputation has caused or become the basis of a political split on the reservation: the conservative faction versus the "militant." Whether or not a person is sympathetic with AIM tells others on which side of the political fence that person stands with regard to various issues. AIM's supporters clearly and cogently defend AIM's activities as being the only way to take control over an undesirable situation. AIM's critics blame the organization for nearly every delinquent event that occurs at Rosebud, whether it be a group of people pushing a car into a lake, a fight in a local bar, or a shooting.

Most people at Rosebud feel that their sister reservation—Pine Ridge—is somewhat more traditional than they, and that AIM is more accepted there. They believe that both the elderly traditional and young people who support AIM are usually either Oglala or are from Pine Ridge, or are even from other reservations. AIM members tend to be regarded at Rosebud as "outside agitators," people from the cities who, unsure of their "Indianness," come to the reservation to discover their roots and to stir up trouble.

The overall impact of AIM at Rosebud has been to divide the community somewhat; but the majority of Lakota at Rosebud *are* anti-AIM. Of course, AIM supporters would deny that they are an unpopular minority. But public sentiment is clear: AIM is radical, violent, militant, and unpredictable. As such, it is to be feared. The impact that AIM will have on Rosebud in the future depends on many things, among which are the issues AIM chooses to deal with, the political or legislative changes it accomplishes, and the manner in which its members conduct themselves. But it is unlikely that AIM will either be totally accepted or rejected. More likely its effect on the reservation will be like everything else at Rosebud— highly variable.

9.2   ROSEBUD'S FUTURE: THE PLANS AND THE PROBLEMS

Making any generalizations about Indian life is a difficult if not impossible task. Nearly every aspect of reservation life consists of multiple elements and views, multiple alternatives, paradoxical situations, or conflicting attitudes. As has been demonstrated throughout this ethnography, it is this diversity that is typical of Lakota life. Considering the high degree of variability in all areas of Lakota life, what kind of prediction could one make, or trends can one see? What does the future hold for the Lakota? With uncertainty in the areas of economic funding and job development, language revitalization, alcoholic treatment, and religious observance, what will life be like fifty or one hundred years from now? What goals exist for the Lakota people, and can they be met? Will they survive as a cultural and linguistic entity into the next century? If so, in what condition? Can the future be at all secure?

The economic, political, and social concerns for the Lakota revolve around many variables, the two most important of which are jobs and alcohol. The instability and lack of continuity in local government, county, state, and federal programs has wreaked havoc on Indian economic security. This condition, occurring in a population suffering the devastating effects of acute alcoholism, has created an environment of insecurity about the future and of helplessness in dealing with it. The combined impact of economic instability with alcoholism is a cycle of failure that the Lakota are struggling to break.

Without question, the problem of reservation unemployment is a critical one with far-reaching implications. Insufficient jobs perpetuates a welfare economy, with its companion feelings of dependency, resentment, and bitterness about the lack of control over one's life. Perhaps this is why so many Lakota choose the Commodity Foods Program over accepting county welfare Food Stamps: people feel they are entitled to the federally funded Commodity foods, but accepting welfare is looked down upon by the dominant society. The lack of jobs on the reservation causes many young people, who might otherwise contribute their energies toward the improvement and upgrading of reservation living standards, to leave Rosebud in search of financial security. Young people who receive advanced education and training sometimes do return home and take important jobs in the tribe. But others leave and become "urban Indians," hoping to find an existence that, if not equally satisfying, is at least more financially secure. For those who choose to remain at Rosebud, job prospects are not good. As of 1979, the unemployment rate at Rosebud was over 65 percent. With a national unemployment rate of 7 to 12 percent, the statistics for Rosebud spell a grim outlook. Because half the jobs available on the reservation are ultimately funded by the government (with either country, state, or federal monies), fluctuation or inconsistency in the allocation of resources or in the planning and execution of these programs leaves employees vulnerable and uncertain about how long they will have a job. Since the tribe, as a political entity, controls funds for nearly every economic program that creates jobs on the reservation, political instability is a real threat. Programs that once had funding (and long-range goals of job training) are often not renewed, thereby terminating jobs and training programs and hopes for permanent employment. The perpetual dream of economic stability is reflected in this statement by Robert Burnette, former chairman of the Rosebud Sioux Tribe:

> On nearly every reservation there is a group of Indians striving to develop business enterprises which will enable Indians to work on their own land and increase their buying power. One example is the Lakota Cooperative Association on the Rosebud reservation. This business venture will eventually become an entire shopping complex, owned, operated and enjoyed by Indians. The Broad Arrow Investment Corporation, headed by Charles N. Bellow, is primarily responsible for funding this dream. Under construction at present is a garage employing Indian mechanics, to be operated in conjunction with a coffee shop, gift shop, and Indian arts and crafts shop. There are plans to set up a reservation-wide grocery chain as soon as capital is available, and an Indian-made product will be manufactured for nationwide delivery. If the general public would invest in such small business instead of blindly mailing checks to groups making unproved claims, they could buy a piece of the American Indians' brighter future. (Burnette and Koster 1974:103–104)

Unfortunately, the dream envisioned by Burnette never was realized. There is no shopping complex, much less one owned by Indians. There is no reservation-wide grocery chain and no Indian-made product. After Burnette's term as chairman expired, his plans were shelved and replaced by new ones developed by a newly elected administration.

Many of the economic enterprises that are short-lived or fail totally do so because of a firm's inability to obtain sufficient contracts. Between 1974 and 1979, two projects that lost their funding and were subsequently terminated were Lakota Products and Rosebud Electronics. Lakota Products, a local furniture company, met its death because it could not get sufficient contracts to stay in operation. One division of the company manufactured tables, while the second division, a laminating plant, furnished tabletops. Failure in one section of the operation had to result in failure for the other. When contracts were not obtained (such as to make furniture for the U.S. Post Office or Army), the plant laid off dozens of employees. During this time, the unemployment rate on the reservation soared to 78 percent. But when contracts were again obtained, some employees had already found work elsewhere or were unwilling or unable to return. Although some believe the failure of this program was due to "poor management"—that is, overdependence on government contracts and the lack of pursuit of funding elsewhere—the cause for failure is a moot point. Continual changes in local political organization cause a shifting in priorities and methods, and for such businesses, lack of continuity spells failure. Similarly, Rosebud Electronics was making components for IBM, but scarcity in the type of wire employed resulted in a cutback and subsequent lack of work.

The failure or instability of various economic ventures on the reservation is due to several factors, the most important of which is the instability of the local reservation government. Every two years when a new tribal chairman is elected, the plans that the former chairman and his or her administration drew up are often abandoned by the new administration, which has its own plans and ideas for solving unemployment. The shift in administration is a shift in plan and progress, for the old plan loses its impetus and a new one begins. This shift works against the creation of stable, tribally owned business.

Another problem with industrial development lies in the red tape of government bureaucracy—in other words, getting the funds allocated by the federal government into the programs that local reservation residents require. Funds that Congress appropriates for use in "economically depressed areas" are channeled through the Department of Commerce and Economic Development Administration in Washington until they are, at last, placed in the hands of the Regional Office for Indian Affairs (for Rosebud, this branch is located in Denver). This office has its own list of what it considers to be of utmost economic priority, and funding for tribal projects is likely only if the tribe's plans coincide with the needs that the regional office has identified. Sometimes they coincide. But in cases where they do not, the tribe knows it cannot request funds for projects *it* feels are essential if the regional office is sympathetic to others. Consequently, if any funding is to be obtained at all, it must be in areas designated as important by the regional office and not by the tribe itself.

What is the solution to this perpetual problem of economic instability? One part of the solution is, of course, better management and better training of the personnel who will be making managerial decisions. Above all, continuity in economic planning from one tribal administration to the next tribal administration must be achieved. But continuity between administrations requires that political candidates agree on issues and how problems should be solved, and are willing to work together. Such agreement is nearly in violation of the American spirit of cutthroat political battles, in which one candidate gains popularity and support by criticizing the achievements, or lack of them, of the other.

In addition to the cycle of economic instability, there is another failure cycle that prohibits Indian management and ownership of individual or tribal business. This is the lack of experience or expertise that most Lakota suffer in the business world, which is a self-fulfilling prophecy: inability to gain experience *keeps* people from being eligible to gain the experience they need. One woman I knew who supported herself and her family by making quilts wanted to purchase a local motel that was up for sale. Although she applied for a special grant and loan designed specifically to assist Native Americans get started in Indian-owned or -managed businesses, she was refused the grant because of her lack of experience in management. Although she had agreed to pursue management training, the funding agency did not feel that her skills would be sufficient to enable her to run a business. Today, she is still sewing for a living. This type of situation extends to *all* areas of reservation life: if one does not already *have* the experience and skills necessary to a certain profession, gaining them without leaving the reservation is practically impossible. For some, emigration from the reservation is a workable solution. But for the woman just mentioned and many others like her, a move with her dependent children would have been impossible. Indian people are continually faced with such choices—to leave home, family, and culture to pursue western skills, or to remain at home, with few skills and little hope of professional or economic advancement. For many, the price of disassociation from home, kin, and culture is one that they are unwilling and often unable to pay.

Poverty and the lack of jobs often contribute frustration and feelings of helplessness and impotence. Although unemployment does not by itself *cause* alcoholism, the mixing of the two ingredients creates a deadly combination—deadly because once one has gotten caught up in the cycle of not having a job and drinking, the two elements work together to perpetuate each other. Breaking out of the cycle becomes a near impossibility. Having a job part of the time may provide enough money to meet people's immediate financial needs, but, certainly in a typical family in which one adult works to support six or seven individuals, money does not go very far. Many live at a poverty level and have a rather bleak outlook on life. When a large paycheck does arrive, what is not spent on groceries and the household may be spent on alcohol. In a cultural environment in which little recreation or entertainment is available, drinking becomes a favorite pastime for many young and quite a few middle-aged and old people. Weekend drinking is regarded by most Lakota as an inevitable activity over which they have little control. When people have no money, drinking sprees are rare. But on payday, people celebrate; young people especially gather in groups and "go on a toot," often lasting the entire night or an entire weekend. Come Monday, some do not make it back to work, resulting in their being fired. Worse yet, their non-Indian employers accuse them of "drinking up their paychecks" and not valuing their jobs. In the future, these non-Indian employers may prefer not to hire Indians, claiming that they are unreliable and are not serious about keeping their jobs. The result is that the already scarce jobs become even scarcer. And the racial prejudice, already rampant, develops into bitter hatred.

Drinking is considered by some to be a standard part of reservation life, but the extent of the damage it does and the progress it inhibits are not really understood. Deaths from car accidents, exposure, and cirrhosis are only one dimension of the tragedy. The *real* tragedy is the pain of day-to-day life in a family where one or several members are severely alcoholic and cannot keep a job. People are becoming increasingly aware of the need "to do something" about Indian alcoholism, and programs such as Alcoholics Anonymous as well as others have begun to meet with partial success. But the rate of alcoholism is so high that these efforts are considered by many only a "drop in the bucket."

In situations where children observe heavy drinking among their parents and older siblings, they learn that while drinking may not be approved of, it is *accepted*. They learn patterns of drinking: they learn that drinking relieves frustration and furnishes entertainment as well as excuses.

One possible way of dealing with alcoholism in the adult population is to educate young people in schools about the effect of alcohol. Young people who gain a more technical and professional knowledge of the devastating consequences alcohol can have on their lives are far more likely to avoid self-destructive behavior.

The result would be an increase in control over their lives, the necessary first step in making plans and decisions about one's future.

In the last decade, the term "Indian self-determination" has come to represent the current goal of most Native Americans. Self-determination means a lot of things to different people. To the Lakota, it means control over one's life, ability to make decisions that concern one's future, ability to plan for and meet one's needs, and the ability to implement the ideas that would result in a higher and healthier standard of living. All this is a goal that can be set only with the condition that native life not be sacrificed in the process. But true independence and control requires education, physical and mental health, consistency in planning, and a cooperative, sympathetic, and supportive set of government institutions. All the solid planning in the world will be fruitless without government support. And, until now, many have felt that the commitment and support of the federal government for Native Americans has been token and insincere. The problems of unemployment and alcoholism *are* two of the major issues that must be faced in the plans for Indian self-determination. But there are other concerns as well, such as language retention, education, and health.

The native culture, at present, continues to thrive in the homes of some Lakota. For others, economic assimilation is the key to success. No matter what route the Lakota choose, they will only have the means to achieve their goals—the creation of dignity and independence in a distinctively Lakota culture—if they receive, first, the assistance and support necessary to gain control over their lives. Then, self-determination can cease being a goal and start being a reality.

References cited

ABERLE, DAVID F.
  1966   *The Peyote Religion Among the Navajo.* Chicago, Ill.: Aldine Publishing Co.
ANDERSON, JOHN ALVIN
  1971   *The Sioux of the Rosebud: A History in Pictures.* Norman: University of Oklahoma Press.
ANDRIST, RALPH K.
  1964   *The Long Death: The Last Days of the Plains Indian.* New York: Macmillan Co.
BALLAS, DONALD
  1970   "A Cultural Geography of Todd County, South Dakota, and the Rosebud Sioux Indian Reservation." Ph.D. dissertation, University of Nebraska, Lincoln.
BROWN, JOSEPH EPES
  1971 (1953)   *The Sacred Pipe: Black Elk's Account of the Seven Rites of the Oglala Sioux.* Baltimore, Md.: Penguin Books.
BUECHEL, EUGENE
  1970   *A Dictionary of the Teton Dakota Sioux Language.* Pine Ridge, S.D.: Holy Rosary Mission.
BURNETTE, ROBERT, AND JOHN KOSTER
  1974   *The Road to Wounded Knee.* New York: Bantam Books.
CARTER, RICHARD T., JR.
  1966   "Contemporary Shamanism Among the Teton Dakota: A Plains Manifestation of the Conjuring Complex." Master's thesis, University of Nebraska, Lincoln.
Code of Federal Regulations (25 CFR, Part 151)
  1978   *South Dakota Legal Services Newsletter* (October).
DELORIA, VINE, JR.
  1969   *Custer Died for Your Sins.* London: The Macmillan Co., Collier-Macmillan Ltd.
DORSEY, JAMES OWEN
  1894   "A Study of Siouan Cults," in *11th Annual Report of the Bureau of American Ethnology, 1889–90.* Washington, D.C.: Government Printing Office.
FERACA, STEPHEN E.
  1963   *Wakinyan: Contemporary Teton Dakota Religion. (Studies in Plains Anthropology and History, No. 2.)* Browning, Mt. Museum of the Plains Indian.
FISHMAN, JOSHUA
  1972   *Language in Sociocultural Change.* Stanford, Ca.: Stanford University Press.

"Ghost Dances in the West." *The Illustrated American*
   1891   Reprinted. Ramona, Ca.: Acoma Books, 1976.

GROBSMITH, ELIZABETH S.
   1974   "Waku^{n}za: Uses of Yuwipi Medicine Power in Contemporary Teton Dakota Culture." *Plains Anthropologist* 19 (May).
   1976   "Lakota Bilingualism: A Comparative Study of Language Use in Two Communities on the Rosebud Sioux Reservation." Ph.D. dissertation, University of Arizona, Tucson.
   1979a "The Lakhota Giveaway: A System of Social Reciprocity." *Plains Anthropologist* 24 (May).
   1979b "Styles of Speaking: An Analysis of Lakota Communication Alternatives." *Anthropological Linguistics* 21 (October).
   1981   "The Changing Role of the Giveaway in Contemporary Lakota Life." *Plains Anthropologist* 6 (February).

HASSRICK, ROYAL B.
   1964   *The Sioux: Life and Customs of a Warrior Society*. Norman: University of Oklahoma Press.

HERTZBERG, HAZEL W.
   1971   *The Search for an American Indian Identity: Modern Pan-Indian Movements*. Syracuse, N.Y.: Syracuse University Press.

HOLDER, PRESTON
   1970   *The Hoe and the Horse on the Plains: A Study of Cultural Development among North American Indians*. Lincoln: University of Nebraska Press.

HYDE, GEORGE E.
   1974 (1961)   *Spotted Tail's Folk: A History of the Brule Sioux*. Norman: University of Oklahoma Press.

KEMNITZER, LUIS
   1970   "The Cultural Provenience of Objects used in Yuwipi: A Modern Teton Dakota Healing Ritual." *Ethnos* 1:4.

Lakota Woonspe Wowapi
   1973   Rosebud, S.D.: Sinte Gleska College Center.

MACGREGOR, GORDON
   1946   *Warriors Without Weapons: A Study of the Society and Personality Development of the Pine Ridge Sioux*. Chicago: University of Chicago Press.

OLSON, JAMES A.
   1965   *Red Cloud and the Sioux Problem*. Lincoln: University of Nebraska Press.

PAIGE, DARCY
   1979   "George W. Hill's Account of the Sioux Sun Dance of 1866." *Plains Anthropologist* 25 (May).

PIKE, WILLIAM
   1972   *Indian History and Culture*. Pierre, S.D.: Indian Education–Johnson O'Malley Program, Freeman, S.D.: Pine Hill Press.

POMMERSHEIM, FRANK
   1977   *Broken Ground and Flowing Waters: An Introductory Text With Materials on Rosebud Sioux Tribal Government*. Aberdeen, S.D.: North Plains Press.

POWERS, WILLIAM K.
   1977   *Oglala Religion*. Lincoln: University of Nebraska Press.
   1978   "Dual Organization at Pine Ridge." Unpublished manuscript.

Rosebud Sioux Tribe
   1971   Tribal Ordinance.
   1976   Tribal Ordinance No. 76-02.

Sinte Gleska Community College.   n.d. Pamphlet.

South Dakota Legal Services Newsletter
  1978   August, October.
SPICER, EDWARD H.
  1969   *A Short History of the Indians of the United States.* New York: D. Van
          Nostrand.
TAYLOR, ALAN AND DAVID S. ROOD
  1972   *University of Colorado Lakota Project,* Boulder.
UTLEY, ROBERT M.
  1963   *The Last Days of the Sioux Nation.* New Haven, Ct.: Yale University
          Press.
WALKER, J.R.
  1917   "The Sun Dance and Other Ceremonies of the Oglala Division of the
          Teton-Dakota." *Anthropological Papers of the American Museum of
          Natural History.* Vol. 16, Part 2. New York.

Recommended reading

BROWN, JOSEPH EPES
1971   *The Sacred Pipe: Black Elk's Account of the Seven Rites of the Oglala Sioux.* Baltimore, Md.: Penguin Books.
This is an excellent and detailed account of the traditional Lakota religion that describes the actual rituals, their symbolism, meaning, and functions.

FERACA, STEPHEN E.
1963   *Wakinyan: Contemporary Teton Dakota Religion.* Studies in Plains Anthropology and History, Number 2. Browning, Mt.: Museum of the Plains Indian.
This study focuses on the traditional healing and curing rituals *(yuwipi)*, while also providing a modern discussion of the Sun Dance, peyotism, and Christianity.

HASSRICK, ROYAL B.
1964   *The Sioux: Life and Customs of a Warrior Society.* Norman: University of Oklahoma Press.
This book deals in great depth with nearly all aspects of traditional Lakota culture, from the values around which native life was oriented, to the military societies, dress, childhood education and experiences, the role of the horse and warfare, and cosmology. An excellent introduction to Lakota life and culture as it was during the precontact period.

HYDE, GEORGE E.
1961   *Spotted Tail's Folk: A History of the Brule Sioux.* Norman: University of Oklahoma Press.
This book provides a detailed account of the travels and migrations of the Brule bands of Lakota, their arrival and settlement on the Plains, their political life, and the struggles that the society underwent as the Sioux faced reservation life in the late 1800s.

MCFEE, MALCOLM
1972   *Modern Blackfeet: Montanans on a Reservation.* New York: Holt, Rinehart and Winston.
Although not about the Sioux, this is a modern study of another Plains tribe and how they have adapted their traditional culture to fit into contemporary society.

NURGE, ETHEL, ed.
1970   *The Modern Sioux: Social Systems and Reservation Culture.* Lincoln: University of Nebraska Press.
This anthology of readings covers a wide range of topics that all center around modern Sioux peoples: economics, diet and nutrition, cultural identities, and music and dance.

POMMERSHEIM, FRANK
1977   *Broken Ground and Flowing Waters: An Introductory Text, with Materials on Rosebud Sioux Tribal Government.* Aberdeen, S.D.: North Plains Press.
   Written by an attorney, this book focuses on the modern government structure of the Rosebud Sioux, the legal history between the tribe and the federal government, and legislation affecting the Lakota today. The author provides a copy of various important legislative acts, as well as the Constitution and By-Laws of the Rosebud Sioux Tribe.

POWERS, WILLIAM K.
1977   *Oglala Religion.* Lincoln: University of Nebraska Press.
   By focusing on the religion of the contemporary Oglala at Pine Ridge, the author examines traditional beliefs and ritual as they are expressed in relation to the social structure and social life of the Sioux.

WAX, MURRAY L., ET AL.
1964   *Formal Education in an American Indian Community.* Supplement to Social Problems, 11 (Spring).
   An in-depth study of the cultural factors affecting the quality of education among the Oglala at Pine Ridge.

Case Studies in Native North America
edited by George and Louise Spindler

Basso, Keith H. THE CIBECUE APACHE   Pre- and post-reservation society, power, and religion; quotes from people. 1970/106 Pages/ISBN: 0-03-083171-7

Downs, James F. THE NAVAJO   Pastoral economy and ecology, families and their herds, farming, change. 1971/136 Pages/ISBN: 0-03-085483-0

Downs, James F. THE TWO WORLDS OF THE WASHO: An Indian Tribe of California and Nevada   History, nomadic household, ecology, adaptation to the "sad new world." 1966/113 Pages/ISBN: 0-03-056610-X

Dozier, Edward P. HANO: A Tewa Indian Community in Arizona   Kinship and social network, religion and ritual, intercultural relations. 1965/104 Pages/ISBN: 0-03-055115-3

Dozier, Edward P. THE PUEBLO INDIANS OF NORTH AMERICA   Pueblo culture, history, current minority status. 1970/224 Pages/ISBN: 0-03-078745-9

Garbarino, Merwyn C. BIG CYPRESS: A Changing Seminole Community   Contemporary ethnography, changes, introduction of cattle industry, decision making. 1972/132 Pages/ISBN: 0-03-086672-3

Grobsmith, Elizabeth S. LAKOTA OF THE ROSEBUD: A Contemporary Ethnography   The complex, adapting culture of a contemporary reservation community. 1981/144 Pages/ISBN: 0-03-057438-2

Hoebel, E. Adamson THE CHEYENNES: Indians of the Great Plains, Second Edition   Ceremonials, governance, legal system, war, world view, and personality. Three new chapters have been added that tell what has happened to the Cheyenne since the "ethnographic present" of the original classic ethnography. 1978/148 Pages/ISBN: 0-03-022686-4

Jones, David E. SANAPIA: Comanche Medicine Woman   Study of the last surviving Comanche Eagle Doctor and her medicines. 1972/107 Pages/ISBN: 0-03-088456-X

McFee, Malcolm MODERN BLACKFEET: Montanans on a Reservation   Indian-oriented and white-oriented adaptations. Why assimilation has not occurred. 1972/134 Pages/ISBN: 0-03-085768-6

Opler, Morris E. APACHE ODYSSEY: A Journey between Two Worlds   Autobiography of a Mescalero Apache born in 1880, incipient shaman, adaptation to cultural transition. 1969/301 Pages/ISBN: 0-03-078905-2

Rohner, Ronald/Rohner, Evelyn C. THE KWAKIUTL: Indians of British Columbia   Contemporary versus "Potlatch Period" Kwakiutl culture. 1970/111 Pages/ISBN: 0-03-079070-0

Spindler, George/Spindler, Louise DREAMERS WITHOUT POWER: The Menomini Indians   Cognitive organization and adaptive strategies in five contemporary groups. 1971/208 Pages/ISBN: 0-03-085542-X

Spindler, George NATIVE NORTH AMERICANS: Four Cases   Four previously published CSCA covering most important culture areas of native North America— *Hano: A Tewa Indian Community in Arizona; The Kwakiutl: Indians of British Columbia; Modern Blackfeet; Montanans on a Reservation; The Menominee.* 1977/512 Pages/ISBN: 0-03-018401-0

Trigger, Bruce G. THE HURON: Farmers of the North   Reconstruction of Huron culture as a working system. 1969/130 Pages/ISBN: 0-03-079550-8

Underhill, Ruth PAPAGO WOMAN   Study of culture evolution from 1830's to 1970's, based on autobiographical account. 1979/160 Pages/ISBN: 0-03-045121-3

Wolcott, Harry F. A KWAKIUTL VILLAGE AND SCHOOL (CSEC)   A lone school and teacher. School/culture conflicts. 1967/132 Pages/ISBN: 0-03-061775-8